A READER'S COMPANION IV

3,500 Words and Phrases Avid Readers Should Know

by

John L. Bowman

1

John L. Bowman

A Reader's Companion IV

DEDICATION

*This book is dedicated
to all writers of the world*

John L. Bowman

The cover is the classic painting *The Sacrifice of Polyxena* by Le Brun which is a depiction from the ancient Roman poet Ovid showing a compliant Polyxena a being led to her death at a sacrificial alter to appease the war hero Achilles. It captures the artistic ideals of seventeenth-century French academic painting with its choreographed composition, intense facial expressions, and dramatic bodily gestures. (Source- Picryl, https://picryl.com/media/the-sacrifice-of-polyxena-by-giovanni-battista-pittoni-getty-center-556893)

ACKNOWLEDGEMENTS

The 3,500 words and phrases in this book are taken from a variety of sources: word books, dictionaries, encyclopedias, word of mouth, books, various readings, my computer and conversations. They are among the most commonly recurring. Note however, when the meaning of a word or phrase could not be found in the dictionary I sometimes surmised its definition from its roots.

INTRODUCTION

A Reader's Companion IV, 3,500 words and phrases avid readers should know is the fourth in my series of books on words. The first edition was published in 2007, the second in 2014, the third in 2019, and this one in 2024, a span of seventeen years during which I looked up the definition of over 14,000 words. It has been a rewarding effort.

I selected words for these word books for a variety of reasons. The main one was that I simply did not know what a word meant. I sometimes looked up a word because I read it in a different context and discovered its meaning was not what I thought it was. I usually included words that were similar but had different meanings and common words with broader meanings. I like words with interesting contrasts. I sometimes include familiar words because they are from a root word with a less-known meaning. Finally, I included words describing different relations.

Like my other word books, I am not a lexicographer and this is not a scholarly book, but, rather, a brief summary of the definitions of many words and phrases I have encountered in context. Most definitions are brief, abbreviated, and in incomplete sentences. The definitions are not in correct literary or scholastic form. I usually exclude etymology, pronunciation, and root meanings. I occasionally give synonyms and antonyms. I usually ignore the obvious meaning of a word and give only the lesser known one. When words have more than one meaning, I separate them with a semicolon. When words defining one meaning of a word were similar they we separated with a comma. I occasionally included some comments of my own and expanded on a word's meaning. Also, I often add comparison words with '*cf.*' (Latin for confer, compare) that have similar or dissimilar meanings or create an interesting contrast that is found elsewhere in this book. Finally, many of the words are proper nouns for places and persons as well as Latin and literary words and phrases.

I must apologize because there are some words in this book that are in my previous word books. Sometimes I found a better definition, a new meaning, or I just forgot what it meant.

A

A cappella   In music, without instrumental accompaniment.

À cheval   With a leg on each side; astride.

A fortiori   Latin for *from the stronger argument* that is used when drawing a conclusion that is more obvious or convincing.

A mare clausum   A navigable body of water that is under the jurisdiction of one nation and closed to other nations.

à outrance   To the limit, unsparingly; excessive.

A ravir   French for delightfully, beautifully.

A se   Latin for from or by oneself; cf. per se.

Ab aliunde   From some other source, evidence clarifying a document but not derived from the document itself.

Ab extra   Latin from without, from the outside; cf. ab intra.

Ab intra   Latin for from inside, from within; cf. ab extra.

Abaft   In or behind the stern of a ship; nearer the stern of a ship.

Abashed   Embarrassed, disconcerted, or ashamed.

Abatement   Depression.

Abate   To cause to become smaller or less intense; to put an end to or suppress.

Abatis   A defensive obstacle formed by felled trees with sharpened branches facing the enemy.

Abattoir   A slaughterhouse.

Abeyant   Something that is temporarily stopped or inactive; something that is suspended with the possibility of continuing later.

Abide   To accept or act in accordance with a rule or decision; to be able to tolerate someone or something.

Abjure   To solemnly renounce a belief, cause, or claim; cf. adjure.

Ablation   The removal or destruction of an object; the surgical removal of body tissue.

Ablution   The act of washing oneself.

Aborning   Being born or produced.

Abortifacient   That which causes an abortion, especially a drug.

Abracadabra   A word said by magicians when performing a magic trick.

Abrasa tabula   The theory that individuals are born without built-in mental content, and therefore all knowledge comes from experience perception.

Absquatulate   To leave abruptly; to abscond.

Abulia   In psychiatry, the absence of willpower or an inability to act decisively as a symptom of mental illness.

Abysm   A literary or poetic term for abyss.

Acanthus   A herbaceous plant or shrub with bold flower spikes and spiny decorative leaves native to Mediterranean regions.

Acclivity   An upward slope; cf. declivity.

Accoutered   To clothe or equip something noticeably or impressively.

Accretion   The process of growth or increase, typically by the gradual accumulation of additional layers or matter.

Achingly   In a way that arouses or expresses intense sorrow or longing.

Achromatic   Lenses that transmit light without separating it into constituent colors; without color.

Acidulous   Sharp-tasting, sour.

Aconite   A poisonous plant of the buttercup family with pink or purple hooded flowers native to regions of the northern hemisphere.

Acroamatic   Something abstruse, esoteric, and given orally, intended for listeners, often applied to the teachings of Aristotle and his disciples; cf. exoteric.

Acrophobia   Extreme or irrational fear of heights.

Acropolis   A citadel or fortified part of an ancient Greek city, typically built on a hill; c. f. necropolis.

Acrostic   A poem, word puzzle or other composition in which certain letters in each line form a word or words.

Ad captandum   Designed to attract or please the crowd, often used as an argument against emotions.

Ad libitum   Latin for as much or as often as necessary; occurring, used, or distributed as often as necessary or desired; in music with free rhythm and expression; commonly written *ad lib.*

Adamantine   To be adamant; rigidly firm, unyielding; resembling a diamond in hardness or luster.

Adamic   Pertaining to or suggestive of Adam.

Addenda   Additional material added at the end of a book or document to correct, clarify or supplement something.

Adige   The second longest river in Italy that rises in the Alps and empties into the Adriatic Sea.

Adjure   To urge or request solemnly or earnestly to do something; cf. abjure.

Adjutancy   The state or office of being an adjutant, assistant, or helper.

Admeasure   To determine the proper share of; to apportion.

Adolesce   To grow toward maturity; to pass through adolescence.

Adulation   Obsequious flattery; excessive admiration or praise.

Adulterine   Born as a result of an adulterous relationship; illegal, unlicensed, or spurious.

Advection   The transfer of heat or matter by the flow of a fluid, especially horizontally in the atmosphere or the sea.

Adversus Haereses   A commonly used book by Father Irenaeus, Bishop of Lyon, often cited as being against heresies and so-called gnosis.

Advocates diabolic   The devil's advocate; someone who takes a position in an argument that they do not necessarily agree with.

Adze   A tool similar to an axe with an arched blade at right angles to the handle used for cutting or shaping wood; cf. mattock.

Aegis   In classical mythology, a tribute to Zeus or Athena, usually in the form of a goatskin shield.

Aeolian lyre A stringed instrument that produces musical sounds when a current of air passes through it.

Aeolian Relating to or arising from the action of the wind.

Aere perennius Latin for more lasting than bronze.

Aëreal Relating to or occurring in the air or atmosphere.

Aerie A large nest of a bird of prey, especially an eagle, typically built high in a tree or on a cliff.

Aerolite a stony meteorite composed mainly of silicates

Aetiologize The study of causation or origination, the study of the causes, origins, or reasons behind the way things are.

Affettuoso In music, tender or affecting; becoming faster, as if excited.

Affiche A poster, placard or advertisement.

Afflatus A divine creative impulse or inspiration, from Cicero's *De Natura Deorum.*

Agape Wide open (like the mouth), especially in wonder.

Agente A policeman, a police officer.

Agglutinative Having the power to unite or agglutinate; in linguistics pertaining to a language characterized by agglutination such as 'Turkish.'

Aglet The plastic- or metal-coated end of shoelaces.

Agogic   Relating to or denoting an accent produced by lengthening the time value of a note, also called an agogic accent.

Agog   Very eager or curious to hear or see something.

Agone   Archaic for past or bygone.

Agon   Greek for conflict, struggle or contest; a contest in athletics, music, or literature.

Agora   Assembly or market place.

Agraffe   The wired cage that holds the cork in a bottle of champagne.

Ague   Malaria or some other illness involving fever and shivering; a fever or shivering fit.

Ahasuerus   The king of ancient Persia known to the Greeks as Xerxes; Biblical prince, head, chief.

Aide Mémoire   An aid to the memory, especially a book or note; an informal diplomatic message.

Aiguillette   Braided loops hanging from the shoulder of military uniforms.

Akimbo   Hands on the hips and the elbows turned outward.

Al fresco   Done or eaten in the open air.

Alabastine   A wall coating derived from gypsum that was mined from shale beds around Grand Rapids, Michigan.

Alamogordo A city in southern New Mexico where the first atomic bomb was exploded in July 1945.

Albeit Although; in spite of the fact that; however, but.

Alcalde A Spanish administrative official.

Alchemical Relating to or characteristics of alchemy.

Aleph The first letter of the Hebrew alphabet.

Alienist A psychiatrist who assesses the competence of a defendant in a court of law; former term for a psychiatrist.

Allocution A formal speech giving advice or a warning.

Allopathic The treatment of disease with conventional means or with drugs having the opposite effect to the symptoms; cf. homeopathic.

Alma Tademas Lawrence Alma Tadema was a Dutch Victorian classical revivalist painter.

Almeh A learned woman.

Almshouse The poorhouse.

Aloe A succulent plant with fleshy leaves and bell-shaped flowers native to Old World tropics often used as ornaments; a strong laxative made from the bitter juice of aloe.

Alpaca A long-haired domesticated South American mammal related to the llama, valued for its wool.

Alpenstock A long, iron-tipped staff used by hikers and mountain climbers.

Alphanumeric Using both letters and numerals.

Alsatia A district in London that was a sanctuary for debtors and lawbreakers.

Alter et idem Another of the same kind.

Altissimus Most high, highest; deep, profound.

Altitude Great height.

Amain Archaic for at full speed; in great haste.

Amatory Relating to or induced by sexual love or desire.

Ambraciot An ancient Greek people that inhabited the borders of Ampilochia.

Ambulation The act of moving about or walking.

Ambuscade An ambush.

Amerce In old English law, to punish with a fine.

Amerind Relating to the indigenous peoples of the Americas.

Amethyst A precious stone consisting of a violet or purple variety of quartz.

Amethystine A purple or violet form of transparent quartz used as a gemstone; a moderate purple to grayish reddish purple.

Amma An abbess or spiritual mother.

Amour Courtois A highly stylized code of conduct between lovers that is often the subject of medieval literature.

Amour proper A sense of one's own worth; self-respect.

Amphetamine A drug that stimulates the central nervous system and is used in the treatment of.

Attention deficit Hyperactivity disorder, narcolepsy, and obesity.

Amphibious Related to both land and water.

Amphibrachic In prosody, a metrical foot consisting of a long syllable between two short syllables.

Amphisbaena A mythological, ant-eating serpent with a head at each end.

Amphorae A tall, ancient Greek or Roman jar with two handles and a narrow neck.

Amphoteric In chemistry, a compound molecule or ion that can react both as an acid and base.

Amplitudinously A raised platform for impromptu speeches; bulky, large, broad, chunky or portly.

Amritsar syndrome A metabolic syndrome involving a cluster of conditions that increase the risk of heart disease, stroke and diabetes.

Amygdala The region of the brain associated with emotional processes, derived from a Greek word meaning almond due to the structure's shape.

Anagram A word, phrase or name formed by rearranging the letters of another, such as *cinema* formed from *iceman.*

Analogue A person or thing seen as comparable to another; relating to information represented by continuously variable quantity such as spatial or position.

Ananias Club A euphemism used by American Press in 1906 to refer to public figures accused of dishonesty, rather than saying 'liar.'

Ananias A habitual liar or prevaricator from a Biblical character.

Anapaests A metric foot characterized by two short syllables followed by a long one.

Anapestic In formal poetry, a metrical foot consisting of two short or unstressed syllables followed by one long or stressed syllable.

Anatomie French for anatomy, which is derived from the Greek words for up and cutting.

Anaximander's dictum 'But whence things take their origin, thence always precedes their passing away, according to necessity; for they pay one another penalty (*dike*) and retribution (*tisis*) for their wickedness (*adikia*) according to established time.'"

Andalusia Spanish for *to walk easily.*

Andamans Relating to the Andaman Islands, an archipelago in the Bay of Bengal.

Andaman Islands An Indian archipelago in the Bay of Bengal and Myanmar, whose capital city, Port Blair, has a jail named for its myriad of small cells meant for solitary confinement.

Andax Hindu for *personal style.*

Anemone A plant of the buttercup family typically bearing brightly colored flowers distributed wildly and popular as garden plants.

Aneroid A barometer that measures air pressure by the action of the air in deforming the elastic lid of an evacuated chamber.

Angelus A Roman Catholic devotion commemorating the incarnation of Jesus and including the Hail Mary said at morning, noon and sunset.

Angularity The quality of having sharp points.

Anhedonia The inability to gain pleasure from normally pleasurable experiences.

Aniconic Symbolic or suggestive rather than literally representational; not a likeness; aniconic religion is one that does not use images or idols.

Aniline   A colorless, oily liquid present in coal tar used in dyes, drugs and plastics.

Anima mundi   The soul of the world; there is an intrinsic connection between all living things like the soul is connected to the human body.

Animadversion   Criticism or censure; a comment or remark, especially a critical one.

Animadvert   To criticize or censure; to speak out against.

Animalcule   A microscopic animal.

Anise   A Mediterranean plant of the parsley family cultivated for its aromatic seeds which are used in cooking and herbal medicine.

Anneal   To heat and then cool, usually for softening and making less brittle; to cool slowly.

Annus mirabilis   A remarkable or auspicious year.

Anode   An electrode of a polarized electrical device through which conventional current enters the device; cf. cathode.

Anodyne   Something not likely to provoke dissent or offense; inoffensive, often deliberately so; a painkilling drug or medicine.

Anon   Soon; shortly.

Anorak A waterproof jacket with hood, usually seen in polar regions; a studious or obsessive person with unfashionable solitary interests.

Antaeus In mythology, an African giant who was invincible when in contact with the earth but was lifted into the air by Hercules and crushed.

Antediluvian Belonging to the time before the biblical flood; ridiculously old-fashioned.

Anteroposterior Relating to or directed toward both front and back.

Anthemion An ornamental design of alternating motifs resembling clusters of narrow leaves or honeysuckle petals.

Anthracite Coal of a hard variety that contains relatively pure carbon and burns with little flame and smoke.

Anthropophagy Man-eater, cannibal.

Anthropose Greek for *human, humanity*.

Antinomian A person who maintains Christians, due to divine grace, are freed from both biblical and moral law.

Antinomianism A person holding antinomian beliefs; cf. antinomian.

Antinomian The view that Christians are released by grace from the obligation of observing the moral law; cf. antinomianism.

Antinous Priceless, inestimable or praiseworthy.

Antiphlogistic A hypothetical combustible substance once thought to be in all matter.

Antiphon A short chant in Christian ritual, sung as a refrain.

Antipodal Diametrically opposed to.

Antipodean In geography, a point on earth that is diametrically opposite to it, connected by a straight line running through the center of the earth; for inhabitants of the northern hemisphere relating to Australia and New Zealand.

Antiquarian Relating to or dealing in antiques or rare books; a person who studies or collects antiques.

Antiquary A person who studies or collects antiques; an antiquarian.

Antiscorbutic Having the effect, like a drug, of preventing or curing scurvy.

Antitetanic Preventing or alleviating muscular contractions, such as in tetanus.

Antithetical Pertaining to antithesis or opposition of words and sentiments, contrasted.

Antitussive A drug used to prevent or relieve a cough; cf. Dionine.

Antmire Archaic for *an ant*.

Apace Swiftly, quickly.

Apellor   A person who prosecutes; obsolete for a person who accuses another in a criminal appeal.

Apercus   A comment or brief reference that makes an illuminating or entertaining point.

Aphelion   The point in the orbit of a planet, asteroid or comet at which it is furthest from the sun.

Aphorism   A pithy observation that contains a general truth.

Apocalyptic   Describing or prophesying the complete destruction of the world.

Apocryphal   Of doubtful authenticity, although widely circulated as being true.

Apocryphon   A secret book.

Apologue   An allegorical narrative usually intended to convey a moral.

Apostasy   An act of refusing to continue to follow a religious faith; abandonment of a previous loyalty; a defection.

Apostrophe   A literary device that refers to a speech or address to a person who is not present or to a personified object.

Apothecaries profit   Something uncommonly extravagant.

Apotheosize   To elevate (to the rank of god); to idolize.

Apotropaic   Supposedly having the power to avert evil influences or bad luck, e.g. apotropaic magic.

Appogiatura   A grace note performed before a note of the melody and falling on the beat.

Apposition   The relationship between two or more words or phrases in which the two units are grammatically parallel and have the same referent; the positioning of things or the condition of being side by side or close together.

Apricity   The warmth of the sun in winter.

Apricot   An orange-yellow color.

Apron   A small area adjacent to another larger area or structure.

Apropinquity   The state of not being close to someone or something; proximity; cf. propinquity.

Apropos des bottles   Without any reason or motive.

Apse   A large semicircular or polygonal recess in a church arched or with a domed roof, typically at the eastern end and usually containing the altar.

Apse   A semicircular niche in a church.

Aqua mala   Bad water in Spanish.

Arabesque   An ornamental design consisting of intertwined flowing lines originally found in Arabic or Moorish decoration.

Arabic or Moorish decoration   A posture in which the body is supported on one leg with the other leg extended horizontally backward.

Araby   An archaic or poetic name for Arabia.

Aramaic   A Semitic dialect used in the Near East from the 6th Century BC that gradually replaced Hebrew as the Jewish language.

Arborescent   Resembling a tree in growth or appearance.

Archaistic   The use of archaic diction or style.

Architectonic   Relating to architecture or architects; the scientific study of architecture.

Architrave   A main beam resting across the tops of columns, specifically the lower third entablature; the molded frame around a doorway or window.

Archly   To act in a roguish, sly, or mischievous manner; to imply you know more about something than someone else.

Arch   To be clever or crafty.

Argent   Silver, silvery white; silver as a heraldic tincture.

Argonaut   In Greek mythology, a band of heroes sailing with Jason in quest of the Golden Fleece; an adventurer engaged in a quest; a small floating octopus with webbed, sail-like arms.

Argos   A city in the Peloponnese, Greece that is one of the oldest continually inhabited cities in the world.

Argotic   A special vocabulary and idiom of a particular profession or social group.

Argufy   To argue.

Ariadne's Thread   Ariadne was a Cretan princess in Greek mythology associated with mazes and labyrinths, Ariadne's thread means solving problems by multiple means such as a physical maze, a logic puzzle or an ethical dilemma through the application of logic to all available routes.

Armoire   A wardrobe or movable cabinet, typically one that is ornate or antique.

Armorial   Relating to heraldry or heraldic devices.

Armscye   The armhole in clothes where the sleeves are sewn.

Arpeggioe   The notes of a chord played in succession, either ascending or descending.

Arriviste   An ambitious or ruthlessly self-seeking person, especially one who has recently acquired wealth or social status.

Arroyo   A steep gully formed by fast-flowing water in an arid region, found mostly in the southwestern United States.

Ars poetica   A poem that explains the art of poetry; a meditation on poetry using the form and techniques of a poem.

Arsis   A stressed syllable or part of a metrical foot in Greek or Latin verse.

Artifact   An object made by a human being, typically an item of cultural or historical interest.

Ary   A thing belonging to or connected with, such as awry.

Asafetida A fetid, resinous gum obtained from the roots of an herbaceous plant used in herbal medicine and cooking; a Eurasian plant of the parsley family from which gum is obtained.

Asdics Later known as sonar, a secret device for locating submerged submarines by using sound waves.

Ashplant A walking stick fashioned from a sapling that has been cut off below the surface of the soil.

Aspection Archaic for the act of viewing, a look.

Asperity Harshness of tone or manner.

Asphodel A Eurasian plant of the lily family, typically having long, slender leaves and flowers borne on a spike; an immortal flower said to grow in the Elysian fields.

Aspic A jelly made with meat stock, set in a mold, and used to contain pieces of meat, seafood, or eggs.

Aspirate To breathe something in, inhale.

Assam A black tea grown in northeastern India.

Assegais A slender, iron-tipped, hardwood spear used chiefly by southern African peoples; a South African tree of the dogwood family that yields hard timber.

Asseverate To declare or state solemnly or emphatically.

Asseveration A solemn or emphatic declaration or statement.

Assiduous   Showing great care and perseverance.

Assignation   An appointment to meet someone in secret, typically made by lovers; the act of assigning or an assessment made.

Aster   A plant of the daisy family that has bright-rayed flowers, typically purple or pink.

Astigmatic   Showing incapacity for observation or discrimination; an astigmatic fanaticism, a disregard for the facts.

Astraea Redux   In Greek mythology, the daughter of Zeus and Themis (justice) who left the earth at the end of the Golden Age and whose reappearance marks the return of justice and a new Golden Age.

Atelier   A workshop or studio, especially one used by an artist or designer.

Athanor   A type of furnace used by alchemists able to maintain a steady heat for long periods.

Atrocitarian   Those who use atrocity stories to demand government action.

Attic   A low story or decorative wall above an entablature or the main cornice of a building.

Au courant   Aware of what is going on; well informed.

Au pair   A foreign person, usually a young woman, who lives with a family and looks after their children or cleans the house in return for meals, a room and a stipend.

Audi alteram partem   Latin for *listen to the other side, or let the other side be heard as well.*

Augean task   An extremely formidable or difficult task that is occasionally distasteful; cf..

Augean   Relating to the mythical king Augeas who is famous for his fabulous stables; cf.
Augean task.

Aught   Archaic for anything at all.

Aural canal   The tubular passage of the outer ear leading to the tympanic membrane; cf. aural.

Aural   Relating to the ear or the sense of hearing; cf. aural canal.

Auratic   Characterized by or relating to an aura; relating to the distinctive quality or essence of a person, work of art, or object.

Aureate   Denoting, made of or having the color of gold.

Auricular   Relating to the ear or hearing; shaped like an auricle or earlobe.

Autocatalytic   Catalysis of a reaction by one of its products; cf. catalysis, hyeterocatalytic.

Autodidactic   A self-taught person.

Automatism   The performance of actions without conscious thought or intention.

Autonomous   Undertaken or carried out without outside control.

Ave verum virginitas   From Ave Maris, hail true virginity.

Axiology   From Greek "value" and "worth," the philosophical study of value.

Ayahuasca   A tropical vine native to the Amazon noted for its hallucinogenic properties.

Azure   Bright blue in color like a cloudless sky.

B

Babel Confused noise made by a number of voices; a scene of noisy confusion.

Bacchic Relating to Bacchus or the worship of Bacchus; drunken and debauched.

Baccy A British informal name for tobacco.

Backslide To relapse into bad ways or error.

Badaliya An Arabic vow of substitution whereas someone offers their life for another, especially a Muslim.

Badinage Playful repartee; banter.

Bafflegab Incomprehensible or pretentious language, especially bureaucratic jargon.

Bagatelle A short, unpretentious instrumental composition; a short, light, and mellow piece of music; a thing of little importance; a very easy task.

Bagnios A brothel, bath house, or prison for slaves.

Baguette A long, thin loaf of French bread that is made from lean dough.

Baize A coarse, typically green woolen material resembling felt used for covering billiard and card tables.

Balaam's Ass In religion, Balaam could curse or bless others and always got from God what he wanted, the story of Balaam and the ass comes when he cursed the Israelites' God who "turned his tongue" so that the curse fell upon his own people and a blessing fell upon Israel.

Balalaika A Russian musical instrument like a guitar with a triangular body and three strings.

Baldaquin (or baldachin) A ceremonial canopy over an altar or throne.

Baldric A belt for a sword or other equipment worn over one shoulder and reaching down to the opposite hip.

Ballantine Celts who worshiped the deity Bal.

Ballotine A dish of meat, poultry, or fish that is stuffed and rolled.

Balsam An aromatic resinous substance, such as balm, exuded by various trees used in fragrances, medicine and cosmetics.

Baluster A short pillar or column typically decorative in design in a series supporting a rail of coping.

Balustrade A railing supported by balusters, especially an ornamental parapet on a balcony, bridge, or terrace.

Banausic Concerning earning a living; relating to ordinary people or ordinary jobs that require technical skills rather than high levels of education; ordinary and not refined.

Bandeau A narrow band worn around the head to hold the hair in position.

Banderole A long narrow flag with a cleft end, flown at a masthead.

Banditti A robber or outlaw belonging to a gang and typically operating in an isolated or lawless area; a bandit.

Bandung Anything that is mixed from other ingredients or comes in pairs.

Bane The cause of great distress or annoyance.

Bann An announcement of an intended marriage, especially in a church.

Bannock device The metallic device used to measure your feet at the shoe store.

Banquette An upholstered bench along a wall, especially in a restaurant or bar; a raised step behind a rampart.

Banshee A female spirit in Irish folklore who heralds the death of a family member, usually by screaming, wailing, shrieking or keening.

Bantle A bunch of stuff.

Banyan   An Indian fig tree whose branches produce aerial roots that later become accessory trunks, sometimes covering several acres.

Baobab   A short tree with an enormous trunk and large, edible fruit that usually lives to a great age.

Barabbas   A condemned criminal pardoned by Pilate to appease the mob that demanded he be freed instead of Jesus.

Barbette   A fixed, armored housing at the base of a gun turret on a warship or armored vehicle; a platform on which a gun is placed to fire over a parapet.

Barbizon   Relating to the school of mid-19th-century French landscape painters whose naturalistic canvases were based on direct observation of nature.

Bardolph   A personal name with Germanic origins meaning *axe* or *wolf* used often by Shakespeare in his plays and once as a thief.

Bark   To rub off or scrape the skin; to girdle; to cover, enclose; a sailing vessel with three or more masts with the fore- and mainmasts rigged square, also called a barque or barc.

Baron   The five ranks of British nobility are, in ascending order, Duke, Marquis, Earl, Viscount and Baron, the Baron who pledges loyalty and service to his superior in return gets land that he can pass to heirs; cf. Duke, Marquis, Earl, and Viscount.

Barque   A sailing ship typically with three masts.

Barrera A red, wooden fence surrounding a building; the first row of seats in the amphitheater of a building.

Basileus A king.

Basilisk A mythical reptile with a lethal gaze or breath hatched by a serpent from a crock's egg.

Basso ostinato In music, a motif or phrase that repeats in the same musical voice and often the same pitch.

Bass Refers to very low sounds.

Bastinado A form of punishment or torture that involves caning the soles of someone's feet.

Bast Shoes made from bast or fiber taken from the bark of trees such as the linden that are basket woven to fit the foot.

Bathing box A small structure for changing clothes at the seaside.

Batrachian A tailless amphibian of the Anura order; a frog or toad.

Batten A long, flat strip of squared wood or metal used to hold something in place or to fasten against a wall; to thrive, prosper, or live in luxury, especially at others' expense.

Baudrillardian Pertaining to Jean Baudrillard, a French sociologist and philosopher; all meaning in society has become meaningless due to mutability; cynicism.

Baulk To hesitate or be unwilling to accept an idea or undertaking.

Bay   A reddish brown color; a shrub.

Bayard   A legendary magic horse renowned for his spirit and supernatural ability to adjust to the size of his riders.

Beadle   A ceremonial officer of a church, college or similar institution; a minor parish officer dealing with petty offenders.

Beaky   Resembling a bird's beak; hooked.

Beard   A person who carries out a transaction, typically a bet, for someone else to conceal the other's identity; a person who pretends to have a romantic or sexual relationship with someone else in order to conceal true sexual orientation; to bodily confront or challenge someone.

Beatific   Blissfully happy.

Beau sabreur   A gallant warrior; a handsome or dashing adventurer.

Beau   A rich, fashionable young man; a dandy.

Beau monde   the fashion world; high society.

Bedad   Used to express surprise or for emphasis.

Bedizen   To dress up or decorate gaudily.

Bedward   Heading toward bed.

Beetling   When something sticks out over the top of something else; a beetling brow is thick eyebrows that stick out from the face.

Beeve   A beef; a beef creature.

Beeves   Plural for beef.

Beglamour   To impress or deceive with glamour.

Begob   By God; a mild oath.

Begorra   An Irish euphemism for *by God.*

Belabored   To argue or elaborate in excessive detail; to attack or assault physically or verbally.

Belaced   To decorate with lace; in nautical terms, to fasten.

Belladonna   A deadly poison prepared from the leaves and root of deadly nightshade containing atropine.

Belles Letters   Beautiful letters; beautiful or fine writing.

Below the salt   A person with low social status.

Bema   The altar part or sanctuary in ancient Orthodox churches.

Benighted   Contemptible intellectual or moral ignorance, usually due to the lack of opportunity; overtaken by darkness.

Benignant   Kindly and benevolent.

Benignity   Kindness or tolerance toward others; an act of kindness.

Benison   A blessing.

Beotch   An affectionate or disparaging form of address.

Berchew   Nicolas Berchew was a 17th-century Dutch painter.

Berg   A mountain, a large mass or a hill.

Bergamot   An oily substance from the rind of the fruit of a dwarf variety of Seville orange tree used in cosmetics and tea flavoring; the tree that bears Seville oranges.

Beribboned   Decorated with many ribbons.

Besotted   Strongly infatuated; archaic for intoxicated, drunk.

Bestia Trionfante   A book by Giordano Bruno consisting of a moral trilogy satirizing contemporary superstitions and vices along with criticism of Christian ethics and in particular the Calvinistic principle of salvation by faith alone.

Bestiaries   A descriptive or anecdotal treatise on various real or mythical animals, especially a medieval work with a moralizing tone.

Bête noire   A person or thing especially disliked or dreaded, bugbear; cf. bugbear.

Betel   The leaf of an Asian evergreen climbing plant used in the East as a mild stimulant; when chewed, it turns the teeth black.

Betimes   Before the usual or expected time, early; sometimes, on occasion.

Bibulous   Excessively fond of drinking alcohol.

Bien trouvés Good, well, okay, right.

Bill of Attainder A piece of legislation that declares a party is guilty of a crime.

Billet doux A love letter.

Bimeby Eye dialect for *by and by*; cf. eye dialect.

Bingle A collision, especially an automobile accident.

Bioscope Chiefly British, a motion picture projector or motion picture theater.

Birched To beat someone with a bundle of birch twigs as a formal punishment.

Birch To beat with or as if with a birch; to whip.

Bishopric A council of three men who work under the direction of the First Presidency to manage temporal affairs.

Bisque Rich, creamy soups typically made with shellfish and especially lobster.

Bitumen A black viscous mixture of hydrocarbons obtained naturally or as a residue from petroleum distillation used for road surfacing and roofing.

Blackamoor A black African or a very dark-skinned person.

Blackcurrant A small, round edible black berry that grows in loose, hanging clusters.

Blackguard Vagrant city children.

Black leg A swindler.

Blancmange A sweet pudding prepared with almond milk and gelatin and flavored with rum or kirsch.

Blare To proclaim loudly and flamboyantly.

Blazon To display prominently or vividly; in heraldry to describe or depict in a correct heraldic manner.

Blepharitis An inflammation of the eyelid that affects the eyelashes and tear production.

Blind pig An illegal drinking place.

Blindworm A slowworm or legless lizard that has very small eyes and a snakelike body that is usually brownish.

Blood horse A thoroughbred or purebred horse bred especially for racing.

Blue Riband A decorative piece of blue cloth that is given to the winner in a contest or competition.

Bluestocking An intellectual or literary woman, often meant derogatorily.

Bluet A low-growing North American plant of the bedstraw family with small, four-petaled flowers and paired leaves.

Boat davit A crane-like device used for raising or lowering boats, anchors, and cargo from the side of a ship.

Bobateria A barber shop.

Bocage Pastureland divided into small, hedged fields interspersed with groves of trees.

Bock A strong, dark beer brewed in the fall and drunk in the spring.

Bodhisattvas In Buddhism, a person who can reach nirvana but delays doing so out of compassion to save suffering beings.

Bodkin A blunt, thick needle with a large eye used for drawing tape or cord through a hem; a long pin used for fastening hair.

Boffin A person engaged in scientific or technical research.

Bogan A deregulatory term for an uncouth or unsophisticated person regarded as being of low social status.

Bole The trunk of a tree.

Bollard A sturdy, short, vertical post originally used to moor a boat.

Bon Marché Cheap.

Bon mot A witty remark.

Bonae voluntatis Peace and goodwill toward men from Gloria in Roman Catholic Mass.

Bonbonièrre A small, decorative box used to contain sweets; confectionery used as a table decoration at formal events or celebrations.

Bonhomie   Cheerful friendliness; geniality.

Boniform   Promoting, perceiving, or akin to good.

Bonito   A smaller relative of the tunas, with dark oblique stripes on the back and important as a food and game fish.

Bonobo   A chimpanzee with a black face and black hair found in the rainforests of the Democratic Republic of Congo.

Boodle   Money, especially that gained or spent illegally or improperly.

Book   To call to account, to investigate.

Boorish   Rough and bad-mannered; coarse.

Bootless   To be ineffectual, useless.

Boots   A hotel servant who cleans boots.

Borean   Greek for northern; a hypothetical linguistic macro family that encompasses northern peoples; cf. hyperborean.

Boric   A white crystalline acid obtained from salt and used as a weak antiseptic and fire   retardant.

Bornin   Obsolete for *to give birth to*.

Borzoi   A large Russian wolfhound with a small narrow head and silky white coat.

Boss   To be excellent, outstanding.

Botticellian Pertaining to Sandro Botticelli, Italian painter of the early Renaissance era.

Bottomry A system of merchant insurance in which a ship is used as security against a loan to finance a voyage; the lender losing the investment if the ship sinks.

Bourbon A reactionary.

Bourne A limit or boundary; a goal or destination.

Bourse A stock market in a non-English speaking country, especially France.

Boutonniere A spray of flowers worn in a buttonhole.

Bowdlerize To remove improper or offensive material, especially if the result is a weaker or less effective test.

Bower A pleasant shady place under trees or climbing plants in a garden or wood.

Bowler A player at tenpin bowling, lawn bowling or skittles.

Bowsprit A spar extending forward from a ship's bow to which the forestays are fastened.

Box tent The tiny plastic table placed in the middle of a pizza box.

Bozart Bad art.

Brabant A historic region of the Low Countries, formerly a duchy of the Holy Roman Empire that is now divided between the southern Netherlands and north-central Belgium.

Brabble To argue loudly.

Bracken A tall fern with coarse lobed fronds, which is found worldwide and can cover large areas; cf. frond.

Brake Break horsepower is the available power of an engine assessed by measuring the force needed to break it.

Brannock The metallic device used to measure feet.

Brasier A large metal container in which coal or charcoal is burned.

Brassica A genus of plant that includes cabbage, turnip, brussels sprout, and mustard.

Bravura Great technical skill and brilliance shown in a performance or activity; the display of great daring.

Brazier A portable heater consisting of a pan holding lighted coals, a barbecue; a worker in iron.

Breadstuffs A cereal product such as grain or flour; bread.

Brevet A military commission conferred for outstanding service with promotion to a higher rank without the corresponding pay; cf. brevetted.

Brevetted To confer a brevet rank on; cf. brevet.

Briarean Relating to or resembling Briareus, a giant said to have a hundred hands; many handed.

Brie A kind of soft, mild, creamy cheese with a firm white skin.

Brigantine A two-masted sailing ship with a square-rigged foremast and a fore-and-aft-rigged mainmast.

Bright's disease An archaic term for nephritis, or inflammation of the kidneys caused by toxins, infection, or autoimmune conditions.

Brilliantine Scented oil used on men's hair to make it look glossy; shiny dress fabric made from cotton and mohair or cotton and worsted.

Brindle A brownish or tawny color of animal fur, with streaks of other colors.

Brio Vigor or vivacity of style or performance.

Brisbanality Platitudinous talking or writing.

Brisket Meat cut from the breast of an animal, typically a cow.

Bristly Having a stiff and prickly texture.

Brobdingnagian Gigantic; a giant, from Johnathan Swift's *Gulliver's Travels,* the fictional land of giants.

Brogan A coarse, stout, leather shoe reaching to the ankle.

Bromo seltzer A compound containing bromide, sodium bicarbonate, etc., used for headaches, upset stomach, and as a sedative.

Broom sedge A species of grass native to the southeastern United States.

Browsing An animal feeding on leaves, twigs, or other high-growing vegetation.

Bruit To spread a report or rumor widely.

Buckler A small round shield held by a handle or worn on the forearm.

Buckra A disparaging term for a white person or person of predominantly white ancestry; a boss, master.

Bugbear A cause of obsessive fear, irritation, or loathing; cf. bēte noire.

Bugger A young male.

Bugle Glass beads.

Bummer Foragers of General Sherman's Union army during its march to the sea through South Carolina.

Bumper A generous glassful of an alcoholic drink, typically one drunk as a toast.

Bumptious Self-assertive or proud to an irritating degree.

Bum Chiefly British; The backside, buttocks.

Bunco A swindle or confidence trick; to swindle or cheat.

Buncombe or **Bunkum** Nonsense.

Bung A stopper for closing a hole in a container; to close with a stopper.

Bung starter A tool for opening barrels by removing the bung; cf. bung.

Bunoa Fortuna Generally good luck, but in some places it means others really don't want the best for you.

Bunyanesque Relating to or suggestive of the allegorical writings of John Bunyan and his tales of lumberjack Paul Bunyan.

Burgeone To begin to grow or increase rapidly; to flourish.

Burin A steel tool used for engraving copper and wood; in archaeology a flint tool with a chisel point.

Burnoose A long, loose hooded cloak worn by Arabs.

Bursar A person who manages the financial affairs of a college or university.

Burschenschaft Associations formed by students to promote patriotism, Christian conduct and liberal ideas.

Busher A major league baseball player who has recently come from a small league.

Buskin A calf-high or knee-high boot of cloth or leather.

Butterbrod A slice of bread topped with butter.

Butterine An artificial butter made partly from milk.

C

Cabalistic Relating to mystical interpretation or esoteric doctrine.

Cabbala A collection of medieval Hebrew manuscripts.

Cabriole A jump in which one leg is extended into the air forward or backward, the other is brought up to meet it, and the dancer lands on the second foot.

Cached To store away to hide or for future use; to store data in a memory.

Cachet Conferring praise; standing or estimation in the eyes of people; having prestige; a design inscription printed or stamped.

Cadaver The medical term for a dead body; a processed dead body; cf. corpse, carcass.

Cadge To ask for or obtain something to which one is not entitled.

Caesurae A break between words within a metrical foot; any interruption or break.

Cagliostro, Alessandro An Italian adventurer and imposter.

Caique A light rowboat used on the Bosporus; a small eastern Mediterranean sailing ship.

Cairngorm Scottish semi-precious stone.

Calaboose A prison.

Calash A jacket hood.

Calcine To reduce, oxidize or desiccate by roasting or applying strong heat.

Calèche A low-wheeled carriage with a removable hood.

Calembours A pun or clever and amusing use of a word or phrase that has two meanings.

Caliban A man of beastly nature, from the monster in Shakespeare's *Tempest.*

Calico A printed cotton fabric; a multicolored or mottled animal, usually a cat.

Calipash and **Calipee** The edible parts of a turtle.

Calla Flowering plants of the arum family, e.g. a lily.

Calomel A white powder used as a purgative and a fungicide.

Calumet A North American Indian peace pipe.

Calvary The place where Jesus was crucified; a sculptured representation of the Crucifixion, usually in the open; an experience or occasion of extreme suffering, especially mental suffering.

Calved To give birth to a calf; when iceberg or glaciers split and shed smaller masses of ice.

Calve To give birth to a calf; to split and shed (as a calving iceberg).

Cambric A lightweight, closely woven white linen or cotton fabric.

Camellia An evergreen eastern Asian shrub grown for its showy flowers and shiny leaves.

Camenae In Roman mythology, nymphs with prophetic powers who inhabit springs and fountains.

Camerado Spanish for comrade; a commercial film production group that makes independent videos and events.

Camisole A woman's loose-fitting undergarment for the upper body, typically held up by shoulder straps and having decorative trimming.

Camlet Tough waterproof clothing.

Campagna Aa low-lying plain surrounding Rome, Italy; once fertile it deteriorated to malarial marshes but since has been reclaimed.

Campanile A bell tower.

Canaan An ancient region lying between Jordan, the Dead Sea and the Mediterranean, a region promised by God to Abraham.

Canapé A small piece of bread or pastry with a savory topping often served with drinks at a reception or formal party; a sofa, especially a decorative French antique.

Canary (in a coal mine) An advance warning of some danger, originating from times when coal miners used caged canaries while working who would die if any methane or carbon monoxide became hazardous to humans; someone acting as an informer or decoy for the police.

Canch A small portion.

Candillo In Spanish regions, a military or political leader.

Canningite A faction of British Tories in the first decade of the 19th century through the 1830s who were led by George Canning.

Canoodle To kiss and cuddle amorously.

Cant A cant hook is a logging tool with a lever handle and hook at one end used for handling and turning logs (cf. peavey); hypocritical and sanctimonious talk, typically of a moral, religious or political nature; language peculiar to a specified group or profession and regarded with disparagement (cf. slang).

Cantatrice A female singer; especially a professional soloist.

Canticle A hymn or chant, typically with a biblical text forming a regular part of a church service.

Cantonment A military garrison or camp.

Canuck Canadian; sometimes used derogatorily.

Canvas back One who gets knocked out a lot, ending up on the ground.

Caoutchouc Unvulcanized natural rubber.

Capital The topmost member of a column or pilaster.

Capote A long cloak or coat with a hood, usually part of an army or company uniform.

Captious Tending to find fault or raise petty objections.

Caput Mortuum Latin for dead head or worthless remains, used in alchemy.

Caracole A half-turn to the right or left performed by a horse and rider.

Caraway The seeds of a plant of the parsley family used for flavoring and oil.

Carbine A light automatic rifle.

Carbonaro In Italy, a secret political society with liberal republican aims.

Carborundum A hard silicon carbide crystal used as an abrasive for cutting, grinding and polishing.

Carcass The dead body of an animal; cf. corpse, cadaver.

Carceral Relating to or suggesting a jail or prison.

Card A mechanical process that disentangles, cleans and intermixes fibers of wool to produce a continuous web or sliver; cf. carder.

Carder A person employed to card wool; cf. card.

Carillon A set of bells in a tower played using a keyboard or by automatic mechanism similar to piano rolls.

Carlist A supporter of Don Carlos as having rightful title to the Spanish throne.

Carlson Scandinavian for a free man; a free peasant settlement.

Carnal Relating to physical, especially sexual, needs and activities.

Carnation A plant of double flowered varieties found in many color variations; moderate red; archaic for the variable color of human flesh.

Carneades A 159 BC academic skeptic born in Cyrene who refuted the dogmatic doctrines of Stoicism and Epicureanism.

Carnelian A semi-precious stone consisting of an orange or orange-red variety of chalcedony; cf. chalcedony.

Carnet A book of tickets for use on public transportation; a customs permit allowing a motor vehicle to be taken across an international border for a limited time.

Carniceria A butcher shop.

Carnsarn A mild oath.

Carpet-eater Slang for someone who eats vagina, one who performs cunnilingus like a lesbian.

Carpo consciente A person who is not a conscious being (compared to an empty mind, open to the deposits of reality from the world outside).

Cartouche A carved tablet or drawing representing a scroll with rolled-up ends used ornamentally or bearing an inscription.

Cascaret A candy used as a laxative for constipation.

Casemate A fortified gun emplacement from which guns are fired in a fortification.

Cassock A full-length garment of a single color worn by Christian clergy.

Castle Building wishful thinking.

Castrati A male singer castrated in boyhood to retain a soprano or alto voice; the practice of castration.

Casus belli An act or situation provoking or justifying war.

Cat's paw A person who is used by another to carry out an unpleasant or dangerous task; a dupe.

Catafalque A decorated wooden framework supporting the coffin of a distinguished person during a funeral or while lying in state.

Catalepsy A medical condition characterized by a trance or seizure with a loss of sensation and consciousness accompanied by rigidity of the body.

Catalpa A tree with large heart-shaped leaves, trumpet-shaped flowers and long seed pods native to North America.

Catalysis The acceleration of a chemical reaction by a catalyst; cf. autocatalytic.

Catamenial Relating to the menses or menstruation.

Cataract A large waterfall; steep rapids and waterfalls in a river, figuratively a cataract of surprises.

Catarrh Excessive discharge or buildup of mucus in the nose or throat that is associated with inflammation of the mucous membrane.

Catastrophe An event causing great and often sudden damage or suffering; a disaster.

Catboat A sailboat with a single mast placed well forward and carrying only one sail.

Catchpenny Having a cheap, superficial attractiveness designed to encourage quick sales.

Catchpoll A sheriff's deputy, especially one who makes arrests for failure to pay a debt.

Caterwaul   To make a shrill howling or wailing noise like that of a cat.

Catherine wheel   A firework in the form of a flat coil that spins when fixed to something solid and lit; in heraldry, a wheel with carved spikes projecting around the circumference.

Cathode   An electrode of a polarized electrical device through which conventional current leaves the devise; cf. anode.

Catholicism   Roman Catholicism, western civilizations, Christian church and spiritual force.

Catonian   Pertaining to or resembling Roman Cato the Elder; severe and inflexible.

Causa sui   Latin for cause of itself or self-caused; denotes something that is generated within itself.

Cavalier   A supporter of King Charles I in the English Civil War; a dashing and attentive man, especially one acting as a lady's escort; a horseman, especially a cavalryman; a small spaniel with long hair and silky coat; showing a lack of proper concern, offhand.

Cave of Adullam   In the Old Testament, the cave in which King David sought refuge from King Saul; a group of seceders from a particular political or intellectual position.

Cavil   To make petty or unnecessary objections.

Caw   The harsh sound of a crow or similar bird.

Cayenne A pungent, hot-tasting red powder prepared from ground dried chili peppers.

Cecrops The mythological founder of Athens.

Celerity Swiftness of movement.

Cellaret A wine cabinet.

Cella The inner area in an ancient Greek or Roman temple typically housing a hidden cult image.

Censer A container in which incense is burned, typically during a religious ceremony.

Centenary The hundredth anniversary of a significant event; a centennial.

Centripetal In physics, moving or tending to move toward a center.

Cerberus In Greek mythology, the multi-headed dog that guards the gates of the Underworld to prevent the dead from leaving, also called the hound of Hades.

Certiorari A writ or order by which a higher court reviews a decision of a lower court.

Chaconne A composition in a series of varying sections in slow triple time, typically over a short, repeated bass theme; a stately dance performed to a chaconne popular in the 18th century.

Chador   A large piece of cloth that is wrapped around the head and upper body leaving only the face exposed, worn especially by Muslim women.

Chafing   Dish, a metal pan with an outer pan of hot water used for keeping food warm.

Chagrin   Distressed or embarrassed at having failed or been humiliated.

Chalcedony   A microcrystalline type of quartz occurring in several forms including onyx, agate and jasper; cf. onyx.

Chaldean   An ancient people who lived in Chaldea c. 800 BC and ruled Babylonia 625-539 BC, renowned as astronomers and astrologers.

Chalmy   Chlamydomonas is a solitary double-flagellated, plant-like algae common to fresh water and damp soil.

Chamomile   An aromatic European plant of the daisy family with white and yellow flowers.

Champarelle   A cocktail made of cognac, anisette and green chartreuse.

Chancel   That part of a church near the altar reserved for the clergy and choir and usually separated from the nave; cf. nave.

Chancery   A court of equity; an office attached to an embassy or consulate.

Chantilly A delicate silk scalloped along one edge, widely used for bridal gowns; a dessert topping of whipped cream, sweetening and usually vanilla flavoring.

Chapfallen With one's lower jaw hanging due to extreme exhaustion or dejection.

Chaplaincy The office or position of a member of the clergy attached to a chapel, institution, ship or branch of the armed forces; the place where a chaplain works.

Chaplet A wreath worn on the head; a string of beads; a part of a rosary; a small carved molding.

Chapultepec Means *at the grasshopper hill* which refers to a large rock formation that is the center of a park's first section.

Charcuterie board An appetizer served on a wooden board featuring meats, cheeses, crackers and bread; cf. Charcuterie.

Charcuterie A French term for a brand of cooking devoted to products like bacon, ham, sausage, terrines, galantines, ballotines, pâtés and confit; cf. charcuterie board.

Charlady Chiefly British; An old-fashioned term for a part-time house cleaner as opposed to a maid who usually lived within the house.

Charnel Associated with death.

Chartism A working-class movement for political reform in the United Kingdom from 1838 to 1857.

Char To burn or reduce to charcoal.

Charybdis   In Greek mythology, the female sea monster who challenged Odysseus.

Chasuble   A sleeveless, outer vestment worn by a Catholic or High Anglican priest celebrating Mass, typically ornate and having a simple hole for the head.

Chaunt   Archaic for chant.

Chaussée   Pavement, a roadway.

Chaussure   Shoes, footgear.

Chautauqua   Iroquois word with multiple meanings including *a bag tied in the middle* and *two moccasins tied together*; any of various traveling shows and local assemblies that flourished in the U.S. in the late 19th century; an institution that provided popular adult education courses and entertainment in the late 19th and early 20th centuries.

Chela   A large pincer-like claw of arthropods like the crab and scorpion.

Cheops   Egyptian Pharaoh of the 27th century BC who commissioned the Great Pyramid at Giza.

Cheroot   A cigar with both ends open and untampered.

Cherubim   A winged, angelic being of the second highest order who attends God.

Chess d'oeuvres   A masterpiece, especially in art or literature.

Cheval glass A tall mirror fitted at its middle to an upright frame so that it can be tilted.

Chevalier A knight; a chivalrous man; a member of certain French orders of knighthood such as the Legion of Honor.

Chevaux de frise A defensive obstacle that exists in many forms and different applications.

Chevron a line or stripe in the shape of a V or an inverted V, especially one on the sleeve of a uniform indicating rank or length of service; zig-zag lines.

Chevy A hunt, chase or pursuit.

Chiaroscuro The treatment of light and shade in drawing and painting.

Chiasmus A rhetorical figure in which words or concepts are repeated in reverse order; e.g. "poetry is the record of the best and happiest moments of the happiest and best minds."

Chiffonier A tall chest of drawers usually with a mirror on top; a low cupboard sometimes with a raised bookshelf on top.

Chilblain A painful, itching swelling on the skin, typically on the hand or foot, caused by poor circulation in the skin when exposed to cold.

Chilbouk A long-stemmed Turkish tobacco pipe with a clay bowl.

Chinch A bed bug.

Chink   A small cleft, slit or fissure; a weak spot that may leave one vulnerable.

Chinkapin   A North American chestnut tree.

Chin   Music idle chatter.

Chintz   Printed multicolor cotton fabric with glazed finished, used especially for curtains and upholstery.

Chipped beef   Smoked dried beef sliced thin.

Chiton   A long, woolen tunic worn in ancient Greece.

Chloral   A colorless, viscous liquid made by chlorinating acetaldehyde used as a sedative and hypnotic substance.

Chlorophyllic   Resembling or derived from chlorophyll.

Choky   Tending to cause choking or to become choked.

Cholera morbus   A gastrointestinal illness characterized by cramps, diarrhea and sometimes vomiting.

Choleric   Bad-tempered or irritable.

Cholmondeley   In Old English, a wood, clearing; a village in Cheshire, England.

Choristers   A member of a choir, especially a child or young person singing the treble part in a church choir; a person who leads the singing of a church.

Chortle   To laugh in a breathy, gleeful way; to chuckle.

Chowder A thick soup.

Chrestomathy A selection of passages from an author or authors designed to help in learning a language.

Christian kabbalah An esoteric, Christian method of discipline and school of thought in Christian mysticism.

Chrome A metal that is used to cover other metals to make them shiny.

Chromo Short for chromolithograph, a colored picture printed by lithography, especially in the 19th and early 20th centuries.

Chryfostom John Chrysostom was an early church father and archbishop of Constantinople known for his denunciation of abuse of authority by ecclesiastical and political leaders.

Chthonic Concerning, belonging to, or inhabiting the underworld; cf. Erinye.

Chuck The part of the forequarter from the neck to the ribs including the shoulder blade.

Churl An impolite and mean-spirited person; archaic for a miser or person of low birth, a peasant.

Churlish Rude in a mean-spirited and surly way.

Chutney A spicy condiment made of fruits or vegetables with vinegar, spices, and sugar, originating in India.

Chyle A milky bodily fluid consisting of lymph and emulsified fats that is formed in the small intestine during digestion.

Chyron An electronically generated caption superimposed on a television or movie screen.

Cincture A girdle or belt.

Cinders The slag from a metal furnace; dross.

Cinephile A person who is fond of motion pictures.

Cinquecento The 16th century period of Italian art, architecture, or literature characterized by a reversion to classical forms.

Cipher A secret or disguised way of writing a code; a zero, the figure O.

Circe In Greek mythology, an enchantress or sorceress renowned for her knowledge of potions and herbs.

Circonstance attenuante French for mitigating circumstances, circumstances that mitigate the seriousness of a crime.

Circumambient Surrounding.

Circumlocution The use of many words where fewer would do, especially in a deliberate attempt to be vague or evasive.

Cirque A half-open, steep-sided hollow at the head of a valley or on a mountainside formed by glacial erosion; a ring, circlet, or circle.

Citron A large, fragrant citrus fruit with a thick rind; a shrubby Asian tree that bears large fruits similar to lemons, but with flesh that is less acidic and peels that are thicker and more fragrant.

Civis Romanus Latin for *I am a Roman citizen*, from Cicero pleading for the legal rights of a Roman citizen, especially when traveling.

Civitas Dei *The City of God* written by Augustine of Hippo as a Christian philosophy against the pagans in the early 5th century AD.

Claddagh An Irish design of two hands holding a crowned heart that symbolizes friendship, loyalty, and love.

Clangorous Making a continuous loud banging or ringing sound.

Clapper A percussion instrument with long, solid pieces that are struck together to produce a sound, like the metal piece inside a bell that it strikes to make a sound.

Claque A group of sycophantic followers; a group of people hired to applaud or heckle a performer or public speaker.

Clavier A keyboard instrument, especially one with strings, such as a harpsichord.

Cleft Past of cleave; to split or divide into two.

Clerestory In architecture, a high section of a wall that contains windows above eye level to admit light and/or fresh air.

Clew   The lower or after corner of a sail; the cords by which a hammock is suspended.

Clientela paradox   Juvenal refers to this paradox in ancient Rome's client-patron sexual custom, called clientela, whereby the ostensible superior patron may themselves have a patron ad infinitum which makes the patron subserviently further down the ladder which makes it a perverted sexual paradox.

Cliquism   The tendency to associate in cliques; the spirit of cliques.

Cloacal   A cavity at the end of the digestive tract for the release of both excretory and genital products in vertebrates.

Cloaca   The posterior orifice that serves as the only opening for the digestive, reproductive and urinary tracts of many vertebrate animals.

Clodhopper   A large, heavy shoe; a foolish, awkward or clumsy person.

Cloisonné   A decorative work in which enamel, glass or gemstones are separated by strips of flattened wire placed edgeways on a metal backing.

Clove   A ravine or rocky fissure; a gorge.

Cloven hoof   A divided hoof common to sheep and goats ascribed to a satyr, the god Pan, or to the Devil, sometimes used as a symbol or mark of the Devil.

Coadunate   The union of dissimilar substances in one body or mass; united, joined together.

Coathanger A clothes hanger.

Cob A hazelnut or filbert, especially one of a large variety.

Cockade A rosette or knot of ribbons worn on a hat as a badge of office or party.

Cock-a-hoop Extremely and obviously pleased, especially about a triumph or success.

Cockatoo A parrot with an erectile crest found in Australia and eastern Indonesia.

Cockchafer A large, brown European beetle that flies at dusk and is often called a Maybug or Maybeetle.

Cockcrow Dawn.

Cockney A dialect of the English language mainly spoken in London by working-class and lower-middle-class people; a demonym for a person from the East End of London, born within earshot of Bow Bells; cf. demonym.

Cocotte A small, heatproof dish in which individual portions of food can be cooked and served; high-class prostitutes in France in the 1860s.

Code duello A set of rules for one-on-one combat, or duel, intended to regulate dueling and prevent vendettas between families.

Codon In biochemistry, a sequence of three nucleotides which together form a unit of genetic code in a DNA or RNA molecule.

Codpiece   A usually conspicuous and decorative pouch attached to a man's breeches to cover the genitals, worn in the 15th and 16th centuries.

Coeval   Having the same age or date of origin; a person of roughly the same age as oneself; contemporary.

Coffer   A strongbox or small chest for holding valuables; a recessed panel in a ceiling.

Coglione   Italian slang for testis, balls; an idiot or prick.

Cognate   A word that has the same linguistic derivation as another, a word from the same original word or root; related, connected.

Cognomen   In ancient Rome, an extra personal name or nickname that is usually passed from father to son; a nickname.

Cognominal   A family name, a surname; one bearing the same name, a namesake.

Cognoscenti   People who are especially well informed on a particular subject.

Coin   To inflict the same kind of injury or ill-treatment that was received from another, hence the expression *out for the coin.*

Colander   A perforated bowl used to strain off liquid from food, especially after cooking.

Colchis   In Greek mythology, a fabulously wealthy land located on the mysterious periphery of the heroic world.

Colewort Ancient word for cole, a brassica, especially cabbage, kale or rape.

Colitis An inflammatory reaction in the colon, often autoimmune or infectious.

Collagist One who makes collages or has made a specific collage; in the manner of a collage, or the making of a collage.

Collectanea Passages, remarks and other pieces of text collected from various sources.

Collier A ship used for carrying coal; a person who carries or sells coal.

Colliery A coal mine and the buildings and equipment associated with it.

Colloid A mixture in which one substance of dispersed insoluble particles are suspended throughout another substance.

Colloquia An academic conference or seminar.

Colloquial Language used in ordinary or familiar conversation; not formal or literary; cf. demotic.

Colloquy à deux A high-level serious discussion between two people.

Collywobbles Stomach pain or queasiness; intense anxiety or nervousness, especially with stomach queasiness.

Coloratura Elaborate ornamentation of a vocal melody, especially in opera.

Columbiad A form of seacoast cannon that is long and chambered, designed to launch shots with heavy charges of powder at high angles.

Columella nasi The space between your nostrils.

Comestible An item of good food; edible.

Comfit A candy consisting of a nut, seed, or other center coated in sugar.

Comité A committee.

Comity An association of nations for their mutual benefit; courtesy and considerate behavior toward others.

Comminatory Threatening, punitive or vengeful.

Commissary Restaurant in a movie studio, military base, prison or other institution; a deputy or delegate.

Committal The burial of a corpse.

Commode Furniture containing a concealed chamber pot; a toilet; a chest of drawers or chiffonier popular in the 18th century.

Comorbidity In medicine, the simultaneous presence of two or more medical conditions in a patient.

Compline Evening prayers in Christianity, traditionally chanted before retiring for the night.

Compounder A person who mixes or combines ingredients to produce animal feed, medicine, or other substance.

Compromit   To put to hazard by some indiscretion; to endanger; to compromise.

Concavity   The quality or state of being curved inward; cf. convexity.

Concentric   Denoting circles, arcs or other shapes which share the same center, the larger often completely surrounding the smaller.

Conceptuses   The embryo in the uterus, especially in early pregnancy.

Concertina   A small, usually polygonal musical instrument played by stretching and squeezing between the hands to work bellows that blow air over reeds; c.f. concertinaed.

Concertinaed   To extend, compress, or collapse in folds like those of a concertina; cf. concertina.

Conche   A machine used in the preparation of chocolate.

Condign   Appropriate to the crime or wrongdoing; fitting and deserved.

Condominium   The joint control of a country's or territory's affairs by other countries.

Condottiere   The leader of a troop or mercenaries, especially in Italy.

Confederate   People or nations united with others as allies; an accomplice, especially in a mischievous or criminal act; anyone who supports you and works toward the same goal with you.

Confit Duck or other meat cooked slowly in its own fat.

Conflagrative That which conflagrates, such as an extensive fire that destroys much land or property.

Congener A thing or person of the same category as another; a minor chemical that gives distinctive character to wine or liquor.

Congeries A disorderly collection; a jumble.

Congiarium An ancient Roman vessel containing one congius, a measure of volume equal to six sextarii.

Congregré malgré Despite congress.

Conjunctive Serving to join; connective; a word or expression acting as a conjunction; cf. disjunctive.

Connemara A hardy pony originally from Ireland and typically gray.

Conning To rob by the use of trickery or threats.

Conniption A fit of rage or hysterics.

Consilience The idea that evidence from independent, unrelated sources can converge on strong conclusions.

Consociationalism A state with major internal divisions along ethnic, religious or linguistic lines, but remains stable due to consultation among the elites of these groups.

Console A central control panel for a mechanical, electrical or electronic system.

Consols Government securities.

Conspectus A summary or overview of a subject.

Constellate To cluster together.

Consubstantial Of the same substance or essence (especially in the Christian Trinity, *Christ is consubstantial with the Father*).

Consumption A wasting disease, especially pulmonary tuberculosis.

Contemn To treat or regard with contempt.

Contralto The lowest female singing voice.

Contrapuntal In music, of or in counterpoint; cf. counterpoint.

Contravallation A series of works confronting the walls of an invested place to isolate the defenders and safeguard the besiegers against sallies.

Contretemps An inopportune or embarrassing occurrence or situation; a dispute or argument.

Contronym A single word with two contradictory meanings.

Contumacy Stubborn refusal to obey or comply with authority, especially a court order or summons.

Contumely Insolent or insulting language or treatment.

Conversazione A scholarly social gathering held for discussion of literature and the arts.

Convexity The quality or state of being curved outward; cf. concavity.

Cooee A cry to attract attention or give a warning; within hailing distance; not approachable.

Coomb A short valley or hollow on a hillside or coastline.

Coppice An area of woodland in which the trees were cut back to stimulate growth.

Copse A small group of trees.

Copula A connecting word, especially as in the form of the verb *be* connecting a subject and complement.

Copulatory To engage in sexual intercourse.

Coquille A dish of scallops usually served with wine sauce.

Corbel A projection jutting out from a wall to support a structure above it; cf. oriel.

Corbleu A crow or raven.

Corded Bound, fastened or wound with cords; twilled or corded fabric; a tense muscle that stands out.

Cordillera A group of parallel mountain ranges along with intervening plateaus.

Cordite   A smokeless explosive made from nitrocellulose, nitroglycerine and petroleum jelly, used in ammunition.

Cordon sanitaire   A guarded line preventing anyone from leaving an area infected by a disease; a measure designed to prevent the spread of undesirable influences; a chain of small states around a larger dangerous hostile state.

Cordon   A line or circle of police, soldiers or guards preventing access to or from an area or building; in architecture, a raised horizontal band or course of bricks on a building, a stringcourse; cf. stringcourse.

Cordovan   A soft horsehide leather from Cordova, Spain.

Corn dodger   A cake of cornbread that is fried, baked or boiled as a dumpling.

Cornpone   Rustic, unsophisticated.

Corona   A rarefied gaseous envelope of the sun and other stars normally visible during a solar eclipse and seen as a pearly glow around the moon; a small circle of light seen around the sun or moon; a part of the body resembling a crown.

Corot, Jean-Baptiste Camille   A French landscape and portrait painter.

Corpsbruder   A comrade in a German student corps; a close comrade.

Corpse   The dead body of a human; cf. carcass, cadaver.

Corpus delicit In law, the facts and circumstances of a crime such as concrete evidence like a corpse.

Corpus juris Latin for *body of law*; the title of a large, encyclopedic collection of laws.

Correggio Antonio Correggio was a foremost 16th-century painter of the High Italian Renaissance known for vigor and sensuousness.

Corrugate To contact or cause to contract into wrinkles or folds.

Corrugation A ridge or groove of a surface that has been corrugated.

Cortege A solemn procession, especially for a funeral; a person's entourage or retinue.

Coruscate To flash or sparkle, as in light.

Corvée A day's unpaid labor owed by a vassal to his feudal lord.

Cosh A thick, heavy stick or bar used as a weapon; a bludgeon.

Cosmotheism The idea that the entire universe is God.

Costive Constipated; slow or reluctant in speech or action; unforthcoming.

Cotentin Peninsula   A peninsula in Normandy, France that forms part of the northwest coast of France and extends northwest into the English Channel, also known as the Cherbourg Peninsula.

Coterie   A small group of people with shared interests or tastes, especially one that is exclusive to other people.

Cottage ornée   A rustic building of picturesque design.

Cotton   To begin to realize or understand something; to begin to like someone or something.

Couchant   An animal lying with the body resting on the legs and the head raised.

Couchant   Lying (like an animal) with the body resting on the legs and the head raised.

Coulee   A deep ravine; a lava flow.

Coulter   The vertical cutting blade fixed in front of a plowshare.

Countenance   To support; to admit as acceptable or possible.

Counterpane   A bedspread.

Counterpoint   In music, playing melodies in conjunction with another according to fixed rules; an argument, idea, or theme used to create a contrast with the main element; cf. contrapuntal.

Counterscarp   The outer wall of a ditch in a fortification.

Coup d'oeil A glance that takes in a comprehensive view.

Coup de grace A final blow or shot given to kill a wounded person or animal.

Coup de main A sudden surprise attack, especially one made by an army during war.

Coup de théâtre a sudden sensational turn in a play; a sudden dramatic effect or turn of events; a theatrical success.

Couped To be confined to a small space.

Covalent Chemical bonds formed by the sharing of electrons between atoms.

Cove A man or person generally preceded by an adjective as in "an old cove."

Coverlet A bedspread, typically less than floor-length.

Covert A thicket in which game can hide.

Cowslip A European primula with clusters of dropping fragrant yellow flowers in the spring that grows on grassy banks and pastures; any of a number of herbaceous plants.

Crabbed Ill-humored, gruffly or sullen; in handwriting, ill-formed and hard to decipher.

Crab In rowing, an accident when a rower's oar gets caught by the water and the handle flies backward into their head or chest.

Crape A lightweight fabric of silk, cotton or other fiber a with finely crinkled or ridged surface worn as a token of mourning; a thin light delicate pancake.

Crapulence The sick feeling you get after eating or drinking too much.

Cravat A necktie.

Craven Contemptibly lacking in courage, cowardly; cf. poltroon.

Cravenette To make a textile water-repellent.

Crèche A model representing the scene of Jesus Christ's birth usually displayed at Christmas; a nursery where babies and young children are cared for during the working day.

Credo quia absurdum Latin for *I believe because it is absurd or impossible*, often attributed to Tertullian.

Crenelate To provide a wall or building with battlements.

Crenellate To create a wall or building with battlements.

Crenulated Having an irregularly wavy or serrate outline; cf. serrate.

Crêpe A light, thin fabric with a wrinkled surface; a thin pancake.

Cresset A metal container of oil, grease, wood or coal burned as a torch and typically mounted on a pole.

Cri de Coeur A passionate appeal, complaint or protest.

Crimination   An accusation of wrongdoing; to charge with a crime.

Crinoline   A stiffened or hooped petticoat worn to make a long skirt stand out; a stiff fabric made of horsehair and cotton or linen thread used for stiffening petticoats.

Cripple pumper   A fire engine that pumps water.

Crise des nerfs   A crisis of nerves; a nervous breakdown; a hysterical fit.

Crispate   Having a wavy or curly edge.

Croaker   A species of marine ray-finned fish.

Crochet   A handicraft in which yarn is made up into patterned fabric by loping yarn with a hooked needle.

Crocket   A small, carved ornament typically a bud or curled leaf on the inclined side of a pinnacle or gable.

Crocus   A small, spring, flowered plant of the iris family with bright yellow, purple or white flowers.

Crofting   A form of land tenure and small-scale food production particular to the Scottish Highlands.

Cropper   A plant that yields a specific crop; a machine or person that cuts or trims something.

Crossbelt   A double belt passing over both shoulders and crossing at the breast to hold sidearms.

Cross -Remainder A situation where land has been willed to two or more people and if one Legatee dies the property goes to the other legatee.

Crotchet A perverse or unfounded belief or notion.

Croupier The person in charge of a gaming table, gathering and paying money or tokens; historically an assistant chairman at a public dinner, usually seated at the lower end of the table.

Crowbait An old horse.

Cruet stand A small stand of metal, ceramic or glass that holds containers for condiments.

Cruller A small cake made of rich, sweetened dough, twisted or curled and fried in deep fat.

Crupper A strap buckled to the back of a saddle and looped under the horse's tail to prevent the saddle or harness from slipping forward.

Crus The lower or hind limb, especially between the knee and the ankle; the shank.

Crypto A person having a secret allegiance to a political creed, especially communism; short for cryptography or the art of writing or solving codes.

Cryptogram A text written in code; a symbol or figure with secret or occult significance.

Cuarantine To quarantine.

Cuarentena A period of approximately 40 days during which a new mother abstains from sex and is solely dedicated to breastfeeding and taking care of her new baby.

Cuban fever Malaria.

Cube steak A cut of beef, usually top round or top sirloin, tenderized and flattened by pounding with a meat tenderizer.

Cūchulainn In Celtic mythology, a heroic warrior who single-handedly defends his country against invaders.

Cuirass A piece of armor consisting of a breastplate and backplate fastened together.

Culebra A tan, dark brown or almost black snake with a pale venter found in Puerto Rico.

Cull To select from a large quantity; to obtain from a variety of sources.

Culm The aerial stem of a grass or sedge, derived from Latin meaning "stalk."

Culotte Women's knee-length trousers cut with very full legs to resemble a skirt.

Cultivar A plant variety that has been produced in cultivation by selective breeding.

Cumbers To hamper or hinder someone or something; a hindrance, obstruction or burden.

Cumin The aromatic seeds of a plant of the parsley family used as a spice, especially as curry powder.

Cumnor A village and civil parish west of the center of Oxford, England.

Cupped To bleed with a cup.

Cupping In Chinese medicine a therapy where heated glass cups are applied to the body creating suction that stimulates the flow of energy.

Cur dues homo From St. Anslem, literal translation is *why God became man.*

Curacao *From Portuguese,* shaped like a heart; a liqueur flavored with the peel of bitter oranges.

Curacy The office, position or work of a curate; cf. curate.

Curate A clergyman; cf. curacy.

Curio A rare, unusual or intriguing object.

Curlicue A decorative or twist in calligraphy or in the design of an object.

Curricle A light, open, two-wheeled carriage pulled by two horses side by side.

Cuspe The point where two curves meet; when one situation ends and another begins.

Cuspidor Probable.

Cuss An annoying or stubborn person or animal; a curse; profanity, cussing.

Customable Subject to the payment of customs.

Cuticura A brand of antibacterial medicated soap or ointment.

Cutwater The forward edge of a ship's prow; a wedge-shaped projection on a pier or bridge that divides the flow of water and prevents debris from getting trapped against the pier or bridge.

Cyanosis A bluish-purple hue to the skin, usually a sign of low levels of oxygen in the blood; cf. cyanotic mouth.

Cyanotic mouth When the lips have a blue tinge; cf. cyanosis.

Cyborg A being that combines organic and inorganic parts.

Cyclorama A circular picture of a 360-degree scene viewed from the inside.

Cyclothymia A mental state characterized by mood swings between elation and depression; bipolar disorder.

Cygnus Latinized Greek word for swan; the northern constellation lying on the plane of the Milky Way.

Cyma A cornice molding with an S-shaped cross-section.

Cypher A secretive, disguised way of writing, a code; obsolete for zero, the figure "O."

Cypress brake A cypress tree that grows in swamps and wetlands.

Cypriote   Relating to Cyprus and its people or culture.

Cyrillic   Denoting the alphabet used by many Slavic peoples.

D

Da capo In music, repeat from the beginning.

Dactyl A foot in poetic meter.

Dado The lower part of the wall of a room, below waist height and usually a differ color or covering from the upper part.

Daedal Skillful, artistic; intricate; adorned with many things.

Daft Silly, foolish; infatuated with.

Dago An Italian, Spanish or Portuguese-speaking person; a pejorative word for an Italian.

Dahabeah A passenger boat used on the Nile, typically with lateen sails.

Dahlgren A smooth-bored gun used by the Union Navy in the American Civil War.

Dalou A relatively large multi-story building; a metal gong idiophone of the Han Chinese.

Dame school A school for neighborhood children by a woman in her own home.

Damon   A legendary figure who pledged his life as a guarantee that his condemned friend Pythias would return to face execution, both of whom were subsequently pardoned.

Damselfly   A slender insect related to the dragonfly, typically resting with the wings folded back along the body.

Damson   A small, purple-black fruit similar to a plum.

Dansant   An informal or small dance.

Darky   An offensive term for a person with black or dark skin.

Dative   Relating to nouns and pronouns that indicate an indirect object; cf. genitive.

Daub   To coat or smear a surface with a thick or sticky substance in a carelessly rough or liberal way; plaster or clay used for coating a surface; a painting executed without much skill.

De gustibus non disputandum est   A Latin maxim meaning "in matters of taste there can be no disputes."

De ipse   Literally, *he himself has said so*, in law it means an allegation is without proof; away by themselves.

De rigueur   Required by etiquette or current fashion.

De te fabula   Latin for *about you the tale is told*.

De trop   Too much or too many; superfluous, excessive.

Dealio Slang or an informal way to say *deal*, e. g. "so here is the dealio."

Deanerie A group of parishes presided over by a rural dean; the official residence of a dean.

Debauched Indulging in or characterized by morally harmful sensual pleasures; dissolute.

Debere Latin for *I ought* or *I must*; to have or keep from someone, to owe something, to be under an obligation for something, the duty to do something.

Decimal Relating to a system of numbers and arithmetic based on the number ten and the powers of ten.

Declaiming To utter or deliver words or a speech in a rhetorical or impassioned way; cf. declamation.

Declamation The act or instance of declaiming; cf. declaiming.

Declamatory Vehement or impassioned expression.

Declension A condition of decline or moral deterioration.

Declivity A downward slope; an area that is lower than surrounding areas; cf. acclivity.

Decolleté A low neckline on a woman's dress or top.

Decrement A reduction or diminution.

Defalcation Archaic for deduction; the act of embezzling; a failure to meet a promise or an expectation.

Defibrillate   To stop fibrillation by administering a controlled electric shock to restore normal rhythm, especially with the heart.

Defilade   The protection of a position, vehicle or troops against enemy observation or gunfire.

Deflagration   The action of heating a substance until it burns away rapidly.

Defrailer   An imaginary device that prevents frailty.

Defrock   To deprive a person of ecclesiastical status; to deprive someone of professional status or membership in a prestigious group; cf. unfrock.

Degauss   To remove unwanted magnetism from a television or monitor to correct color; to destroy the data on a storage device by removing its magnetism.

Degust   To taste carefully.

Dehiscence   The splitting or bursting open of a pod or wound.

Dejure   In law, the rightful entitlement or claim; by right; denoting something or someone that is rightfully such.

Delectare   To obtain pleasure from or take pleasure in something.

Delectation   Pleasure and delight.

Deliciate   To delight oneself.

Delmarva Peninsula The large peninsula on the East Coast
of the United States occupied by Delaware and parts of
Maryland and Virginia.

Démarche A course of action, maneuver; a diplomatic or
political initiative or maneuver.

Deme A political division of Attica in ancient Greece; in
biology, a subdivision of a population consisting of closely
related plants, animals or people, typically breeding mainly
within the group.

Dementia praecox Previously used to describe
schizophrenia, a severe mental disorder with a warped
interpretation of reality.

Demesne Land attached to a manor and retained for the
owner's use; a region or domain; in law, possession of real
property in one's own right.

Demeter's golden sheaf In mythology, Demeter is the
goddess of harvest usually depicted with a sheaf of wheat or
cornucopia in her hands.

Demijohn A bulbous narrow-necked bottle holding 3 to 10
gallons of liquid, typically enclosed in a wicker cover.

Demimonde The class of women considered having
doubtful morality and social standing; any group of people
considered to be on the fringes of respectable society.

Demirep A woman whose chastity is considered doubtful.

Demiurge A being responsible for the creation of the universe (in Platonism, the Creator of the universe, and in other theological systems a heavenly being considered the controller of the material world and antagonistic to all that is purely spiritual).

Demi vierge A girl or woman who behaves in a sexually provocative and permissive way without yielding her virginity.

Demogorgon A mysterious spirit or deity often explained as a primeval creator god who antedates the gods of Greek mythology.

Demoiselle A small, graceful crane with black head and breast and white ear tufts found in southeastern Europe and central Asia; a damselfly.

Demondé Genuinely.

Demonesi A group of nine islands in the Sea of Marmara a few miles southeast of Istanbul.

Demonology The study of demons or demonic belief.

Demonym A noun used to denote the natives or inhabitants of a particular country, state, or city; cf. cockney.

Demotic Denoting or relating to the kind of language used by ordinary people; popular or colloquial; cf. colloquial.

Denaturize To make unfit for drinking by adding toxic or foul-tasting substances.

Dence To be stupid.

Dendrology   The study of trees.

Dengue   A debilitating viral disease of the tropics transmitted by mosquitoes and causing sudden fever and acute pains in the joints.

Denning   To live in or retire to a den.

Denominare   To name, to call.

Dental   Relating to the teeth; in phonetics pronunciation with the tip of the tongue against the upper front teeth (as with th, n, d and t).

Dephlogisticate   To take away the phlogiston, or the ability to burn; to reduce or remove inflammation.

Depilatory   A cream or lotion for removing unwanted hair; something used to remove unwanted hair.

Depraved   Morally corrupt, wicked; cf. deprave.

Deprave   To make someone immoral or wicked; cf. depraved.

Deracinate   To tear something up by the roots.

Derecho   A line of intense, widespread, and fast-moving windstorms and sometimes thunderstorms that move across a great distance often characterized by damaging winds.

Descant   To talk tediously or at length; an independent treble melody usually sung or played above the basic melody.

Descry   To catch sight of.

Desiderata Something that is needed or desired.

Desideratum Something that is needed or wanted.

Despicable Deserving hatred and contempt.

Desuetude A state of disuse.

Detumescence The process of subsiding from a state of tension, swelling, or sexual arousal; cf. tumescence.

Deucalion In Greek mythology, a survivor of the great flood by which Zeus destroys the rest of the human race.

Deuced Devilish; confounded; used for emphasis, especially to express disapproval or frustration.

Deuce The two on dice or playing cards.

Devocion Devotion, devoutness.

Diablerie Reckless mischief, charismatic wildness; archaic for sorcery assisted by the devil.

Diacritical A mark or sign indicating the proper pronunciations of a letter above or below which it is written.

Dialogic Relating to or in the form of a dialogue.

Dialogize To transform into dialogue; to discourse in dialogue.

Diametric Completely opposed, at opposite extremes.

Diapason An organ stop sounding a main register of flue pipes; a grand swelling burst of harmony.

Diarchy A government by two independent authorities.

Diastole The phase of the heartbeat when the heart muscle relaxes and allows the chambers to fill with blood; cf. systole.

Dichoptic Viewing a separate and independent field by each eye (Greek *dicha* meaning two and *optikos* relating to sight).

Diclinous Having the stamens and pistils in separate flowers.

Dicta A formal pronouncement from an authoritative source; a dictum.

Dictograph A telephonic instrument used for secretly listening to or recording conversations.

Didicit Third person for discussion.

Dido A mischievous trick or prank.

Dieppe A fishing port on the Normandy coast of northern France.

Dierne Secret, dark and lamentable.

Dies irae From the Gregorian chant meaning *Day of Wrath* that describes the last judgment of souls before God where some will be saved and go to heaven and others unsaved who will be cast into the eternal flames of suffering.

Diet A meeting of bishops and nobles.

Differentiae   The element that distinguishes one entity from another; a characteristic that distinguishes a species from other species of the same genus.

Dilettante   A person who cultivates an area of interest, such as the arts, without real commitment or knowledge.

Diminuendo   A decrease in loudness.

Diminutives   A shortened form of name, typically used informally.

Dimity   A stout cotton fabric with raised strips.

Dingus   To refer to something one cannot or does not wish to name specifically.

Dint   Force, power, blow or stroke, typically one made with a weapon in fighting.

Diocesan   Pertaining to a diocese; a bishop of a diocese.

Dionine   An opioid analgesic and antitussive known as ethylmorphine; cf. antitussive.

Dioptric   Relating to the refraction of light, especially in the organs of sight or in devices which aid or improve vision.

Diorama   A model representing a scene with three-dimensional figures.

Diotima   One who honors or is honored by Zeus; Diotima of Mantinea is the fictional figure in Plato's Symposium considered the origin of the concept of Platonic love.

Diphthongize   To create a sound formed by the combination of two vowels in a single syllable, in which the sound begins as one vowel and moves toward another (as in loud).

Dipsas   A family of snail-eating snakes; in ancient times a serpent whose bite was thought to produce intense thirst.

Dipsomaniac   An uncontrollable craving for alcoholic liquors.

Diptych   A painting, especially an altarpiece, on two hinged wooden panels which can be closed like a book; an ancient writing tablet consisting of two hinged leaves with waxed inner sides.

Dirigible   Capable of being steered, guided or directed.

Dirigiste   Relating to a system in which the government has a lot of control over a country's economy.

Dirk   A short dagger of a kind carried by Scottish Highlanders.

Discommode   To cause someone trouble or inconvenience.

Discursive   Digressing from subject to subject.

Dished   Having the shape of a dish; concave.

Disingenuous   Not candid or sincere, typically by pretending to know less than what one really does; ingenious.

Disinter   To dig something up, especially a corpse, to exhume; to discover something, usually well hidden.

Disjecta membra Scattered fragments, especially of written work.

Disjunctive Lacking connection; in grammar, expressing a choice between two mutually exclusive possibilities; cf. conjunctive.

Dismaliest Superlative form of dismal, most dismal, causing dejection, blue, disconsolate, gloomy, dreary.

Disme Archaic for dime.

Disport Enjoying oneself, unrestrained frolic; diversion from work or serious matters; recreation or amusement.

Dispraise To censure or criticize someone.

Disquisition A long or elaborate essay or discussion on a particular subject.

Dis Roth childishness To criticize wealthy Rothschild-like people.

Dis To speak disrespectfully or to criticize; disrespectful talk.

Distraint In law the seizure of someone's property in order to obtain payment of money owed, especially rent.

Distrait Distracted or absentminded.

Diti An echoic word used to designate the dot of Morse code; another term for dot.

Diurnal During the day; occurring daily.

Divalent   Having a valence of two.

Diver   A loon.

Diwan   In Islamic societies, a central finance department, chief administrative office or regional governing body; in Islamic societies, a chief treasury official, finance minister or prime minister in some Indian states.

Doctrine   A belief or set of beliefs taught by a church, political party or other groups.

Doddery   Slow and unsteady movement due to weakness in old age.

Dodona   The state of being bright and radiant; an ancient Greek town in Epirus that was a sanctuary and oracle of Zeus.

Doff   To remove an item of clothing, such as a hat.

Dog   A brick that is specially made to bond around internal acute angles.

Doggery   A cheap saloon, a dive.

Dogie   A motherless or neglected calf.

Dog star   The brightest star in the sky.

Dollop   A shapeless mass or blob of something, especially soft food; to add casually without measuring.

Dolorous   Feeling or expressing great sorrow or distress.

Dominie   A schoolmaster; a pastor or clergyman.

Domino A cloak worn with a mask for the upper part of the face at masquerades.

Don In Spanish, a title prefixed to a male forename; a university professor, especially a senior member of a college at Oxford or Cambridge Universities.

Donja A Spanish title prefixed to a woman's given name; a lady or gentlewoman.

Donjon The great tower or innermost keep of a castle.

Donnée A subject or theme of a narrative; a basic fact or assumption.

Donnish Resembling a college don, particularly because of their pedantic, scholarly manner.

Don The faculty of an English university.

Dopaminergic Related to dopamine, a neurotransmitter that increases dopamine activity in the brain used to treat Parkinson's Disease.

Doppelganger A biologically unrelated look-alike or double of a living person often portrayed in literature as a ghostly phenomenon, harbinger of bad luck, or evil twin.

Doric Relating to a classical order of architecture characterized by sturdy fluted columns and a thick, square abacus resting on a rounded molding; relating to the ancient Greek dialect of the Dorians.

Dormouse An agile mouse-like rodent with a hairy or bushy tail found in Africa and Eurasia.

Dorp A small rural town or village.

Doss House A cheap lodging house for homeless people and tramps.

Doss To sleep in rough or inexpensive accommodations.

Douche A shower of water; a device for washing out the vagina; an obnoxious or contemptible person.

Doula A woman, typically without formal obstetric training, who provides guidance and support to a pregnant woman during labor.

Dovecot A shelter with nest holes for domesticated pigeons.

Dow To be able, to prosper, to thrive.

Doxology Praise or glory; in Christianity glorifying God.

Doxological A short hymn or praise to God in various forms of Christian worship, often added to the end of canticles, psalms, and hymns.

Doxologize To give glory to God; to praise.

Doxology A short hymn praising God.

Draft Denoting a beer or other drink that is kept in and served from a barrel or tank rather than a bottle or can.

Dragoman An interpreter.

Dramatis personae The characters of a play, novel or narrative.

Dramaturgy   The theory and practice of a dramatic composition.

Draught   British spelling for draft.

Draughts   The game of checkers.

Draughty   A place, especially a room, that has currents of unpleasant cold air blowing through it.

Dray   A truck or cart for delivering beer barrels or other heavy loads, usually without sides.

Dreidel   A small, four-sided spinning top with a Hebrew letter on each side used in a children's game.

Dropsical   Affected with or characteristic of dropsy; edematous.

Dropsy   An old term for the swelling of soft tissues due to the accumulation of excess water.

Dross   Something regarded as worthless; rubbish.

Drouth   A drought; thirst.

Druze   A member of a religious Islamic sect chiefly in Lebanon and Syria who broke away from other Muslims in the 11th century and are considered heretical by the Muslim community.

Dryasdust   From Sir Walter Scott, a dull, pedantic person; dull and boring.

Ducal   Relating to a dukedom.

Duck A linen canvas once used for sailors' white trousers and outerwear.

Ducks and Drakes To handle recklessly; to squander.

Dude An Easterner in America who goes west.

Dudgeon A feeling of offense or deep resentment.

Duenna An older woman acting as a governess and companion in charge of girls, especially in a Spanish family; a chaperone.

Duff Of very poor quality.

Dug An udder, nipple or teat; refers to suckling animals and in a vulgar sense to women.

Duiker A small African antelope that typically has a tuft of hair between the horns, found mainly in the rainforest.

Duke The five ranks of British nobility are, in ascending order, Duke, Marquis, Earl, Viscount and Baron; Dukes were rulers of provinces; cf. Marquis, Earl, Viscount and Baron.

Dun A dull grayish-brown color.

Dunderpate A stupid or slow-witted person, a dunce.

Duologue A dramatic performance or piece in the form of a dialogue limited to two speakers.

Duology A pair of related novels, plays or movies.

Dur aux grands French for hard times will come and go.

Durance   Archaic for imprisonment or confinement.

Duster   A woman's loose, lightweight full-length coat without buttons originally worn in the 1920s when traveling in an open car.

Dutiable   Liable for customs or other duties.

Dwabliest   A silly defect in language.

Dyadic   The interaction between two things.

Dysania   The condition of finding it difficult to get out of bed in the morning.

E

Earl   The five ranks of British nobility are, in ascending order, Duke, Marquis, Earl, Viscount and Baron, the Earl is in charge of collecting taxes; cf. Duke, Marquis, Viscount, and Baron.

Earwig   A small, elongated insect with a pair of terminal appendages that resemble pincers.

Ebon   Dark brown or black color; ebony.

Ebony   Blackish or very dark brown timber from tropical trees.

Écarté   A card game for two players.

Ecce iterum Crispinus   Latin for *Here's that Crispinus again*, from Juvenal denoting someone who shows up at every event.

Echoic   Of or like an echo.

Echolalia   The meaningless repetition of words occurring as a symptom of mental conditions; the repetition of a child's speech who is learning to talk.

Echt   Authentic and typical, true, genuine.

Eclaircise To make clear; to clear up what is obscure or not understood; to explain.

Eclat Brilliant display or effect; style, flamboyance; social distinction or conspicuous success.

Ectoplasm The viscous, clear outer layer of the cytoplasm of an amoeboid cell; a supernatural viscous substance that is supposed to exude from the body of a medium during a spiritualistic trance.

Edematous A medical term for swelling.

Educe To bring out or develop something; to infer something.

Educt A substance separated from another substance without chemical change.

Efface To erase from a surface; to make oneself appear insignificant or inconspicuous.

Efferent Conducted outward or away from something, e. g. for nerves; the central nervous system.

Effloresce To lose moisture and turn into a fine powder on exposure to air; to reach the optimum stage of development, to blossom.

Egard Regard, consideration.

Eidetic Memory with the ability to see an object soon after you look at it; cf. photographic memory.

Eland   A spiral-horned African antelope that lives in open woodland and grassland, the largest of the antelopes.

Elate   To make someone ecstatically happy; in high spirits; exultant or proud.

Eldorado   A city or country of fabulous riches held by 16th century explorers to exist in South America; a place of fabulous wealth.

Electrolier   A chandelier in which the lights are electrical.

Electrologist   A person who removes unwanted hair on the body using heat and electric current.

Elegiac   Relating to or involving an elegy that expresses mournfulness or sorrow; poetry composed in the form of elegiac couplets.

Elenchus   The Socratic method of eliciting truth by question and answer; especially used to refute an argument; a logical refutation.

Eleusinian Mysteries   Greek initiations for the cult of Demeter considered the most famous of secret religious rites of ancient Greece.

Eleusis   Acceptable or legitimate; sleepy, drowsy; pleasing to the taste, palatable.

Elflock   Tangled hair.

Elicit   To evoke or draw out a response or answer from someone; cf. Illicit.

Elision The omission of a sound or syllable when speaking.

Ellum Good quality sesame oil.

Embolism Obstruction of an artery, typically by a blood clot or air bubble.

Embonpoint Somebody who has a curvy or plump figure; the soft part of a woman's breasts; stoutness.

Embrasure A small opening in a parapet of a fortified building splayed on the inside.

Emetic A medicine or other substance which causes vomiting.

Emigrate To leave one's own country in order to settle permanently in another; cf. immigrate.

Eminence grise A person who exercises power or influence in a certain sphere without holding an official position.

Emolument A salary, fee, or profit from employment or office.

Empathic The ability to understand and share the feelings of another.

Empedoclean Relating to the philosopher Empedocles and his philosophy of change by uniting and dividing forces that act on the elements earth, air, and water.

Emplotment The assembly of a series of historical events into a narrative with a plot.

Emplot   Placing in the context of a plot or storyline.

Emulous   Desiring of equaling or excelling; filled with emulation.

En barbette   A raised fortification; the practice of firing a gun over a parapet rather than through an embrasure.

En brosse   A person's hair cut in a short and bristly style.

En décolletage   A low neckline on a woman's dress revealing cleavage.

En kai pan   One and all, the motto of Comotheism; cf. cosmotheism.

En passant   By the way, incidentally.

En prospectu   A preliminary printed statement that describes an enterprise; something that forecasts the course of nature.

En soi   Being for itself; a mode of existence of consciousness consisting of its own activity and purposive nature.

Encaenia   An annual university ceremony of commemoration with recital of poems and essays and conferring degrees.

Encaustic   *In painting and ceramics*, using pigments mixed with hot wax that are burned in, as an inlay.

Enceinte   Archaic for an enclosure or enclosing wall of a fortified place.

Encincture   To encircle like a girdle; to gird.

Encomiastic Formally expressing praise; a panegyric.

Encoring To give or call for a repeated additional performance at the end of a concert.

Encyclopedist 18th-century French writers identified with the Enlightenment, deism, and scientific rationalism.

Endogenous Growing or originating from within an organism; in psychiatry, a disease not attributable to any external environmental factor; cf. exogenous.

Endymion *In mythology*, the human lover of Selene, goddess of the moon.

Enfant terrible A person whose unconventional or controversial behavior or ideas shocks, embarrasses, or annoys others.

Enfeoffe Under the feudal system, to give someone freehold property or land in exchange for their pledged service.

Engirdle To surround, encircle.

Engirt To envelope, encircle, engrid.

Engouement Infatuation.

Engrid A smart, fair and beautiful girl.

Enoūment Infatuation.

Enragés The small number of ultra-radical firebrands during the French Revolution known for defending the lower classes.

Ens actu An actual being; any kind of existence that is actual; cf. ens potential.

Ens creatum From Descartes, the perfectly sufficient metaphysical substance used to distinguish primary and secondary qualities.

Ens potential A potential being; a being that exists only in the mind; cf. ens actu.

Entablature A horizontal and continuous lintel on a classical building supported by columns or a wall comprising the architrave, frieze and cornice.

Entelechy The realization of potential; the supposed vital principle that guides the development and function of an organism; the soul.

Entente cordiale A friendly understanding or informal alliance between states or factions.

Enteric Relating to the intestines.

Enthralled To capture the fascinated attention of; to enslave; cf. thrall.

Enthymeme An argument in which the premise is not explicitly stated.

Enthymeme An argument in which one premise is not explicitly stated.

Enthymemic *In logic*, an argument in which one premise is not explicitly stated.

Entrainment *In psychology*, the characteristic interactions between brain rhythms and independent oscillatory systems.

Entrain To board a train.

Envenom To impregnate with venom; to make poisonous; to embitter.

Envoi A short stanza concluding a ballade; an author's concluding words.

Envoy A brief ending stanza in literature that serves as a summation or dedication to a particular person.

Ephebian Relating to the youth of ancient Greece; a young man.

Ephelides Freckles.

Epic A long poem, typically derived from ancient oral tradition, narrating the deeds and adventures of heroic or legendary figures or the history of a nation; cf. idyll.

Epiclesis The invocation of one or several gods.

Epicleti In Roman Catholic Mass when transubstantiation occurs or when bread and wine are transformed into the body and blood of Christ.

Epidemiology The study of how diseases spread.

Epidictic The effort to praise or disparage something or someone.

Epigone A less distinguished follower or imitator of someone, especially an artist or philosopher.

Epigrammatic Of the nature or style of an epigram; concise, clever, and amusing.

Epigraphy The study and interpretation of ancient inscriptions.

Epilogue A section or speech at the end of a book or play that comments on or concludes what has happened.

Epimethean In Greek mythology, Epimetheus was the god of afterthought and excuses; foresight.

Epiphyte A plant that grows on another plant but is nonparasitic, such as numerous ferns.

Episcleritis An inflammatory condition of the eye affecting the clear mucous membrane between the inner eyelids and white part of the eye that occurs in the absence of infection.

Episteme True knowledge.

Epithalamium A song or poem celebrating a marriage.

Epithelial Relating to the thin tissue forming the outer layer of a body's surface and lining the alimentary canal and other hollow structures.

Epitomize Archaic for *to give a summary of*, as in a written work.

Epos An epic poem; epic poetry; a collection of poems of a primitive nature handed down orally.

Epworth League   A Methodist young adult association for people aged 18 to 35.

Equerry   An officer of the British royal household who assists members of the royal family; historically, an officer of the household of a prince who had charge over the stables.

Equinoctial   Happening at or near the time of an equinox; another term for celestial equator; at or near the equator.

Equipoise   To balance forces or interests; to balance or counterbalance something.

Erastian   The doctrine that the state is superior to the church in ecclesiastical matters.

Ere   Before in time.

Erechtheum   An ancient Greek temple on the north side of the Acropolis in Athens, Greece, dedicated to both Athena and Poseidon, also known as the portal of the maidens.

Eremite   A Christian hermit or recluse.

Erinye   *In Greek mythology,* also known as furies; female chthonic deities whose special function was to take vengeance on men; cf. chthonic.

Ermine   A stoat, especially when in its white winter coat; cf. stoat.

Ersatz   An inferior substitute for something else; not real or genuine.

Erstwhile   Archaic for former, formerly.

Erysipelas A streptococcal inflammation of the skin.

Erysipelas An acute disease caused by a bacterial infection characterized by large, raised red patches of skin, fever, and severe general illness.

Erythrite A mineral, hydrous cobalt arsenate, that occurs as a powdery, usually red incrustation on cobalt minerals.

Eschatology A part of theology concerned with death, judgment, and the final destiny of the soul and of humankind.

Escritoire A small writing desk with drawers and compartments.

Escutcheon A shield or emblem bearing a coat of arms; a flat piece of metal for protection and sometimes ornamentation around a keyhole, door handle, or light switch.

Esemplastic Molding into one; unifying.

Esopus Archaic spelling of Aesop; a genus of crabs in the family Epialtidae.

Espantoon A police nightstick with an attached strap by which it can be swung.

Espiègle Mischievous.

Espousal The act of adopting or supporting a cause, belief, or way of life; archaic for a marriage or engagement.

Espy To catch sight of.

Essence The intrinsic nature or indispensable quality of something, especially something abstract that determines its character.

Estoppel A legal principle which precludes a person from asserting something contrary to what is implied by a previous action or statement of that person.

Esurient Hungry or greedy.

Etiolate To bleach; to alter development by excluding sunlight.

Etiological Causing the development of a disease or condition; serving to explain something by giving a cause or reason for it, often in historical or mythical terms.

Etiology The study of the causes or reasons for something; in medicine, the causes of a disease.

Etymon A word or morpheme from which a later word is derived; cf. morpheme, morphological.

Eucharist The Christian ceremony commemorating the Last Supper in which bread and wine are consecrated and consumed.

Eu Good, well, easily, normal.

Eumenides *In classical mythology*, the ironic name for *kindly ones* who in reality were hideous snake-haired monsters who pursued unpunished criminals.

Eupeptic Relating to good digestion; having an air of healthy good spirits.

Euphony Pleasing to the ear, especially through a harmonious combination of words.

Euphuism An artificial and highly elaborate way of writing or speaking.

Eurydice In Greek mythology, the wife of Orpheus who tried to bring her back from the dead with his enchanting music.

Evangel The Christian gospel; an evangelist.

Evensong A service of evening prayers, psalms, and canticles.

Eventuate To occur or lead to a result (*overeating eventuates in obesity*).

Evince To reveal the presence of a quality or feeling; to indicate.

Evincive Tending to prove, demonstrative.

Ewer A large jug with a wide mouth used for carrying water for someone to wash in.

Ex gratia Given in payment as a favor from a sense of moral obligation rather than because of any legal requirement.

Ex oriente lux Light from the east, originally referred to the sun rising in the east, but alludes to culture coming from the Eastern world.

Ex post facto Having retroactive effect or force.

Exaction   The action of demanding and obtaining something from someone, especially a payment or service.

Exajoule   A billion billion joules: cf. joule.

Excrescence   A distinct outgrowth on a human, animal or plant body, especially one that is the result of disease; an unattractive or superfluous addition or feature.

Excursus   A detailed discussion of a particular point in a book, usually in an appendix; a digression in a written text.

Execration   The act of cursing or denouncing; something detested.

Exemplum   An example or model, especially a moralizing or illustrative story.

Exfluncticate   To utterly destroy.

Exfoliate   To come apart or be shed from a surface in scales or layers; to remove dead cells from the surface of the skin.

Exfoliation   To shed from a surface in scales or layers; to wash or rub the body to remove dead cells from the skin surface.

Exigent   Pressing, demanding.

Exiguous   Very small in size or amount.

Exogenous   Relating to or developing from external factors; in biology, growing or originating from outside the organism; in psychiatry, caused by an agent or organism outside the body; c. f. endogenous.

Exorta Latin for *having arisen* or *having been born.*

Exoteric Something intended and most likely understood by the general public, especially delivered through speech; cf. acroamatic.

Expatiate To speak or write at length or in detail.

Expectoration To cough up and spit out.

Expend To lay out, spend.

Experimentum crucis *In science*, a crucial experiment.

Expiate To atone for guilt or sin.

Expiation A way to atone for something wrong you did.

Expostulate To express strong disapproval or disagreement.

Expostulation To reason earnestly with a person for purposes of dissuasion or remonstrance.

Expurgatorius Obsolete Latin for books the Roman Catholic Church forbade its members to read unless certain passages (condemned as dangerous to faith or morals) were deleted or changed.

Extern A person working in but not living in an institution, such as a nonresident doctor; cf. intern.

Extrastriate Part of the visual cortex involved in processing specific features of visual information.

Exudation   *In Latin,* to ooze out, the act of exuding, fluid being emitted by an organism through pores such as sweating.

Exuviate   To shed such as skin or a shell.

Ex-voto   A religious offering given to fulfill a vow.

Eye dialect   Intentional misspellings that are based on standard pronunciations intended to show the speaker's illiteracy, e. g. *sez* for *says.*

F

Facetious   Treating a serious issue with inappropriate humor, intending to provoke laughter; flippant.

Factotum   An employee who does all kinds of work.

Factum est   Latin for *it is done*.

Faery   A fairy; imaginary, mystical.

Fag   A tiring or unwelcome task.

Fag end   An inferior and useless remnant of something; a cigarette butt.

Fagged   Extremely tired, exhausted; a student at a boarding school who is required to perform menial tasks for a higher-grade student.

Fagging   To work hard, especially at a tedious job or task.

Faggot voter   A person who is qualified to vote with restricted suffrage only by the exploitation of loopholes in the regulations.

Faggot   A bundle of sticks or twigs bound together as fuel.

Fain   Pleased or willing under the circumstances; compelled by circumstances, obligated; with pleasure, gladly; cf. fane.

Faire valoir   To argue.

Fakir   A Muslim or Hindu religious ascetic who lives solely on alms.

Fallal   A showy ornament, trinket or article of dress.

Fane   A temple or shrine; cf. fain.

Fantasia   A musical composition with a free form and improvisatory style; a musical composition based on several familiar tunes.

Fardel   A bundle.

Farden   A rustic pronunciation of "farthing" (a coin).

Farina   Flour or meal made of several grains, nuts, or starchy roots.

Farrago   A confused mixture.

Farrier   A craftsman who trims and shoes horses' hooves.

Fascicle   A separately published installment of a book or other printed work; in biology, a bundle of structures, such as nerve or muscle fibers.

Fatback   Fat from the upper part of a side of pork, especially when dried and salted in strips.

Fatuity   Weakness or imbecility of the mind; stupidity.

Faugh   Expressing disgust.

Fauns   *In mythology*, the lustful rural gods represented as a man with a goat's horns, ears, legs, and tail.

Fauvism   A style of painting with vivid expressionistic use of color that flourished in Paris around 1905 whose leading figure was Matisse.

Feaze   To become frayed, such as the feazed edges of a coat; to become rough or jagged at the edges.

Febrile   Having or showing the symptoms of a fever.

Feeling intellect (or **Feeling hearts**) from William Wadsworth's poem *Hart Leap Well* which guides us to the way our psychic energy flows.

Felicific   Relating to or promoting increased happiness.

Fellah   An Egyptian peasant.

Fellaheen   A native peasant or laborer in Middle Eastern countries like Egypt and Syria.

Felon   A person who has been convicted of a felony; cruel, wicked; cf. felony.

Felony   A crime, typically involving violence, regarded as more serious than a misdemeanor, and punishable by imprisonment for more than one year or by death; cf. felon.

Felucca   A small vessel propelled by oars or sails in the Mediterranean region.

Fen   A low and marshy or frequently flooded area of land.

Fenian   A member of the Fenian Brotherhood determined to free Ireland from English rule.

Fermé   French for firm.

Ferrule   A typically metal ring or cap that strengthens the end of a handle, stick or tube to prevent it from splitting or wearing; a metal band strengthening or forming a joint.

Fête champêtres   A painting by Giorgione.

Fettle   State or condition of health, fitness, wholeness, spirit.

Feuilletion   A part of a newspaper or magazine devoted to fiction, criticism, or light literature.

Fibula   A brooch or clasp.

Fichu   A small triangular shawl worn around a woman's shoulders and neck.

Fictive   Creating or created by imagination.

Fides and ratio   Faith and reason.

Fidus Achates   A faithful friend or devoted follower.

Fief   A person's sphere of operation or control.

Fiend   An evil spirit or demon; a wicked or cruel person.

Fie   To express disgust or outrage.

Fife   A kind of small shrill flute used with drums in military bands.

Filigree   Ornamental openwork of delicate or intricate design.

Fillet   A fleshy, boneless piece of meat from near the loins or ribs of an animal.

Fillip   Something that acts as a stimulus or boost to an activity.

Finial   A distinctive ornament at the apex of a roof, pinnacle, canopy or similar structure of a building.

Firmament   The heavens or the sky, especially when regarded as a tangible thing.

Fistic   Relating to boxing, pugilistic.

Fistula   An abnormal connection between two body parts, such as an organ or blood vessel, and another structure.

Flagitious   Criminal, villainous.

Flail   A threshing tool consisting of a wooden staff with a short heavy stick swinging from it; to wave or swing wildly; to beat or flog.

Flailed   To wave or cause to wave or swing wildly; to beat or flog.

Flambeau   A flaming torch, especially one made of several thick wicks dipped in wax.

Flaminian Gate A gate on the Aurelian wall through which the road Via Flaminia passed, the principal artery between Rome and Cisalpine Gaul.

Flat-iron A nonelectric iron with a flat bottom heated for use in pressing clothes and cloth.

Flaxen A pale yellow color like dressed flax, especially of hair.

Flechette A type of ammunition resembling a small dart shot from a gun.

Fleshpot Bodily comfort; luxury; places providing luxurious or hedonistic living.

Flews The thick hanging lips of a bloodhound or similar dog.

Flibbertigibbet A frivolous, flighty or excessively talkative person.

Flip-jack A flat cake of thin batter fried on both sides on a griddle; a pancake.

Flitch A slab of timber cut from a tree trunk; the strengthening plate in a flitch beam.

Flog To beat with a whip or stick as punishment or torture; to sell or offer for sale.

Florizel In Shakespeare's *The Winter Tale,* Florizel, son of Polixenes falls in love with Perdita and wants to marry her but his father objects and tells him he will get no inheritance if he sees her again.

Flute   An ornamental vertical groove in a column.

Fob   A chain attached to a watch for carrying in a pocket; a small pocket for carrying a watch; to deceitfully give someone something inferior to what they want.

Foemen   An enemy, foe, or opposition.

Foison   Archaic for a rich harvest; in Scotland, physical energy or strength.

Folio   An individual leaf of paper numbered on the front side only; the page number in a printed book; a sheet of paper folded once to form two leaves (or pages) of a book.

Folly   *In Biblical terms,* to hold the pursuit of truth in contempt by choosing to make our own path.

Fons et origo   The source and origin of something.

Foolscap   A size of paper, now standardized at about 13 X 8 inches.

Fop   A man who is concerned with his clothes and appearance in an affected and excessive way, a dandy.

Foppery   Affected and excessive concern with one's clothes and appearance.

Forelock   A lock of hair growing just above the forehead; the part of the mane of a horse that grows from the poll and hangs down over the forehead.

Forgather   Assemble or gather together.

Forrader To move in a forward direction.

Fortnightly Happening or produced every two weeks.

Foundling An infant that has been abandoned by its parents and is discovered and cared for by others.

Four-flusher Someone who leads you to believe something that is not true.

Fourgon A wagon for carrying baggage.

Fovea The high-resolution center of the retina.

Fox-fire The phosphorescent light emitted by certain fungi on decaying timber.

Fox-grape Any of several native grapes of eastern North America with sour or musky fruit.

Fractal A curved or geometric figure, each part of which has the same statistical character as the whole, like a snowflake.

Fraight Obsolete form of fraught.

Fraktur A German style of black-letter type.

Franchise An authorization granted enabling an individual or group to carry out specific commercial activities; a permit or license; the right to vote.

Frangible Fragile, brittle.

Franking An official mark or signature on a letter to indicate the postage has been paid.

Fraught   Filled with or likely to result in something undesirable; causing or affected by anxiety or stress.

Fraulein   Title for an unmarried German-speaking woman; especially a young woman.

Fretted   Decorated with fretwork, such as a wooden object or structure; cf. fretwork.

Fret   To gradually wear away something by rubbing or gnawing.

Fretwork   An interlaced, usually geometric design that is either carved or cut out, and used as a background, usually of wood or metal; cf. fretted.

Fribble   A frivolous or foolish person; to part with lightly or wastefully, to fritter.

Frijole   Beans in Mexican cooking.

Frill   A projection, such as hair, feathers, bone or cartilage, about the neck of an animal.

Frisson   A sudden strong feeling of excitement or fear; a thrill.

Frock   A woman's dress; a man's double-breasted, long-skirted coat worn chiefly on formal occasions; cf. surtout.

Froe   A cleaving tool with a handle at right angles to the blade.

Frog-looped   Fastenings used on military coats.

Frogged   A coat with ornamental braids or fastenings consisting of a spindle-shaped button and a loop.

Fronde   A sling or catapult.

Frondeur   A political rebel.

Frond   The leaf or leaflike part of a palm, fern or similar plant.

Frontispiece   A false front, a façade.

Fructify   To make something fruitful or productive; to bear fruit or become productive.

Fructile   A gestation process.

Fry   A young, small fish.

Fugato   *In music,* having the style of a fugue.

Fugitive   Quick to disappear; fleeting.

Fugue   In a musical composition when a short melody is introduced by one part and successively taken up by others and developed; in psychiatry, a state of loss of awareness of one's identity, often associated with hysteria and epilepsy.

Fuliginous   Sooty, dusky, obscure, murky; having a dark or dusky color.

Funambulist   A tightrope walker.

Funicular A railroad operated by cable with ascending and descending cars counterbalanced; relating to rope or its tension.

Furbelow A gathered strip or pleated border of a skirt or petticoat; to adorn with trimmings.

Furling The stowing of a boat's sail by flaking, packing, stowing, or rolling.

Furore An outbreak of public anger or excitement; furor.

Furring To block, as in furring up an artery; in construction, to make a surface level by furring or adding strips of material.

Furze A yellow-flowered shrub of the pea family with leaves modified to form spines native to Europe and North Africa, also called gorse.

Fust To become moldy through disuse; to taste or smell moldy or stale.

Futtock Each of the curved timber pieces forming the lower part of a ship's frame.

Fuze Same as a fuse, a device that initiates function, especially as an exploder.

G

Gabardine A smooth, durable twill woven cloth typically of worsted or cotton.

Gaby A Hebrew girl's name meaning *heroine of God.*

Gadding Wandering idly or without aim.

Gainsay To deny or contradict a fact or statement; to speak against or oppose someone.

Gaiter A garment similar to leggings worn to cover or protect the ankle and lower leg.

Galantine A dish of white meat or fish boned, cooked, pressed, and served cold in aspic.

Galled An ancient Gaulish shoe that leaves the ankles bare to show any signs of shackles and slavery.

Gallous Alternative term for gallows.

Gall The contents of the gallbladder; bile; bitterness or bitter tasting.

Galoot A clumsy or oafish person.

Gamaliel Paul sat at the feet of Gamaliel, a highly respected Jewish teacher and leader in Jerusalem, thus it describes a student of another.

Gambetta To dodge, avoid action.

Gambol To run or jump about playfully.

Gamin A street urchin.

Gammon Ham which has been cured or smoked like bacon.

Gandy dancer A track maintenance worker on a railroad.

Ganymede *In Greek mythology*, a Trojan boy who was abducted by gods and ultimately became immortal to be Zeus' cupbearer.

Gaping To stare with open mouth, as in wonder; to open the mouth wide involuntarily as a result of hunger, sleeplessness, or absorbed attention.

Gar A freshwater fish of North America; the garfish.

Garfish Any of a number of long, slender fish with elongated beaklike jaws containing sharp pointed teeth; cf. gar.

Garner To gather or collect, especially information or approval; to store or deposit.

Gar The freshwater garfish of North America; cf. garfish.

Gasconade Extravagant boasting.

Gaucheness   Lacking social experience or grace; not tactful; crudely made or done.

Gaud   A showy and purely ornamental thing.

Gaunilo   A Benedictine monk of Marmoutier Abbey in Tours, France, known for his criticism of St. Anselm's Ontological argument for the existence of God.

Gauntlet   A glove worn with medieval armor to protect the hand; an open challenge such as combat, e.g., to throw down the gauntlet.

Gaur   A large, wild ox native to India and Malaysia.

Gavotte   A medium-paced French dance popular in the 18th century.

Gazetted   To announce or publish something in an official gazette.

Gazpacho   A Spanish-style soup made from tomatoes and other vegetables and spices served cold.

Geas   *In Irish folklore*, an obligation or prohibition magically imposed on a person.

Gelehrten   A female scholar, savant or pundit; a woman of letters; a female academic.

Genial   Friendly and cheerful.

Genii   Plural for genius.

Genitive   Relating to nouns and pronouns that indicate possession or close association; cf. dative.

Genius loci   In classical Roman religion, a protective spirit of a place often presented as a cornucopia, patera or snake.

Gentian   A plant with violet or trumpet-shaped flowers in mountainous temperate regions, cultivated for ornamentation and medicine.

Geomorphology   The study of the physical features of the surface of the earth and their relation to its geological structures.

Geri-chair   The geriatric chair, a large, padded chair designed to help the elderly with limited mobility.

Gesso   A hard compound of plaster of paris or whiting in glue used in sculpture or as a base for gilding or painting on wood.

Gewgaw   A showy thing, especially useless or worthless.

Gibber   To speak rapidly and unintelligently, usually from fear or shock.

Gibbeted   To hang somebody on a gibbet; to execute someone by hanging.

Gibe   An insulting or mocking remark; a taunt.

Gigolo   A young man paid by an older woman to be her escort or lover.

Gill   To gut or clean (a fish); the flesh about the chin or jaws.

Gimel   The third letter of the Hebrew alphabet.

Gimlet   A small T-shaped tool with a screw tip for boring holes; a cocktail of gin and lime juice.

Gingham   A lightweight plain woven cotton cloth, typically checked in white and a bold color.

Giorgione   A 15th-century Italian painter of the Venetian school during the High Renaissance from Venice.

Gitana   A gypsy woman.

Glabella   The space between the eyebrows.

Glacis   A gently sloping bank, especially one that slopes down from a fort exposing attackers to the defender's missiles.

Gladstone   A light portmanteau opening into two equal parts.

Glass-eater   A bad, extra tough person.

Glaucous   A dull grayish-green or blue color; covered with powdery bloom like that on grapes.

Glebe   A piece of land that is part of a clergyman's benefice that provides income; archaic for land, fields.

Glissade   To slide down a steep slope of snow or ice with the support of an ice axe.

Glissando   A continuous slide upward or downward between two notes.

Gnomic   Expressed in short, pithy maxims or aphorisms.

Gnosis   Secret knowledge.

Gnu   A large dark African antelope with a long head, a beard and mane, and a sloping back.

Gobelin   A tapestry made at the Gobelins factory in Paris.

Godhead   God; a greatly admired or influential person.

Goggle-eyed   Having staring or protuberant eyes, especially through astonishment.

Goiter   A swelling of the neck due to enlargement of the thyroid gland.

Golem   *In Jewish legend*, a clay figure brought to life by magic; an automaton or robot.

Goober   A peanut; a foolish person.

Gore   A triangular or tapering piece of cloth forming a part of something as in a skirt or sail; cf. goring, leech.

Gorge   Archaic for the throat.

Gorgonise   To have a paralyzing effect on someone.

Goring   The triangular area along a leech of a square sail created by the presence of a gore; cf. gore, leech.

Gourd   A large fruit that has a hard shell and cannot be eaten; a gourd-shaped necked bottle or flask.

Grackle   A blackbird that looks like it has been slightly stretched.

Grail   A thing that is being earnestly pursued or sought after.

Grandiloquent   Pompous or extravagant in language, style, or manner, especially in a way intended to impress.

Granger   A farmer.

Graphene   Bonded carbon atoms in sheet form one atom thick.

Grass-widower   A man divorced or separated from his wife; a man whose wife is temporarily away from him.

Greave   A piece of armor used to protect the shin.

Greengrocer   A retailer of fruit and vegetables.

Greep   To grasp, clutch.

Griffin   Mythical creature with the head and wings of an eagle and the body of a lion, typically depicted with pointed ears and with the eagle's legs in the place of forelegs.

Griffonage   Illegible handwriting.

Gripes   Gastric or intestinal pain; colic.

Grippe   Archaic term for influenza.

Grip   Traction (or grip) keeps the car on the track, and allows for braking, acceleration and turning.

Groin *In architecture*, the curved edge formed by two intersecting vaults.

Guava An edible, pale orange tropical fruit with pink, juicy flesh and a strong, sweet aroma; the small, tropical American tree that bears the guava.

Guidon A pennant that narrows to a point or fork at the free end, used especially as the standard of a light cavalry regiment.

Gule The throat, the gullet.

Gumbo A French-based patois spoken by some black Creole people in Louisiana; a stew popular in the U.S. state of Louisiana, and is their official state cuisine.

Gumshoe A detective.

Gunrest The wall at the top of the side of a boat; the topmost planking of a wooden vessel; something that rests a gun.

Gurre a l'outrance War to excess, all-out war.

Guttering A candle that has too much melted wax because it is not hot enough to burn readily, so the flame repeatedly goes out, lights again and smokes a lot.

Guyascutis A large, imaginary, four-legged beast with legs on one side longer than on the other for walking on hillsides.

Gyrus A ridge on the cerebral cortex; cf. sulci.

H

Haberteria A haberdashery.

Habiliment Clothing.

Habit A long, loose garment worn by a member of a religious order; dress or attire.

Hagar *According to Genesis*, a concubine of Abraham, driven into the desert with her son, Ishmael, because of Sarah's jealousy.

Hagiography The writing of the lives of saints; derogatory adulatory writing about another person; a biography that idolizes its subject.

Haha A recessed landscape design that creates a vertical barrier while preserving an uninterrupted view of the landscape beyond involving a sharp downward slope to a vertical face.

Halal *In Islamic teaching*, lawful or permitted food; cf. haram.

Halberd A combined spear and battle-axe.

Halcyon *In Greek legend,* a bird usually associated with the kingfisher that was purported to bring peace, prosperity and love.

Hale A strong and healthy person, especially an elderly one.

Hamfatter An inexpert or amateurish performer, especially a mediocre jazz musician.

Hamper A large basket, usually with a cover for packing, storing, or transporting articles.

Hand-lead A small lead for sounding in shallow water.

Hansom A two-wheeled, horse-drawn carriage accommodating two passengers inside with the driver seated behind.

Haplography The inadvertent omission of a repeated letter or letters in writing, e.g. writing *philiogy* for *philology.*

Haram *In Islamic teaching,* unlawful or not permitted food; cf. halal.

Hard Shell-rigid or uncompromising, especially in fundamentalist religious belief.

Hark To listen.

Harlequin A mute character in traditional pantomime, typically masked and dressed in a diamond-patterned costume.

Harmonium A musical keyboard instrument of the reed organ family in which air from pedal-operated bellows causes the reeds to vibrate.

Harpie *In mythology*, a half-human and half-bird monster.

Harrow An implement consisting of teeth and tines that plows.

Haruspices *In ancient Rome*, a religious official who interprets omens by inspecting the entrails of sacrificial animals.

Hasp A lock for a door, window or lid by securing a hasp over the loop of the fastening.

Hatchment A large tablet, typically diamond-shaped, bearing the coat of arms of someone who has died, displayed in their honor.

Hatter A person who makes and sells hats.

Hausfrau A German housewife; a woman regarded as overly domesticated or efficient.

Haut monde Fashionable society.

Hauteur Haughtiness of manner; disdainful pride.

Hawse A part of a ship's bow through which the anchor cables pass.

Hawser A thick rope or cable for mooring a ship.

Hay-barrack An open structure with a moveable roof for storing loose hay on a farm.

Headstock   The part of a guitar that houses the pegs that hold the strings at the head of the instrument, also called a peg head.

Heath   *In Britain*, an area of open uncultivated land with characteristic vegetation of heather, gorse, and coarse grasses; cf. wold, moor.

Hebdomad   The lower regions.

Hebephrenic   A kind of schizophrenia characterized by hallucinations, delusions and silly mannerisms.

Hebraization   To make comfortable to the spirit, character, principles or practices of the Hebrew people.

Hecatomb   In ancient Greece or Rome, a great public sacrifice, originally of a hundred oxen; an extensive loss of life.

Hegira   The migration or journey of the Islamic prophet Muhammad and his followers from Mecca, also called Makkah, a city in western Saudi Arabia, birthplace of Muhammad and spiritual center of Islam; any place people visit or hope to visit.

Heine   Pejorative word for a German.

Helcies   Plural for helix, or a three-dimensional shape like wire wound uniformly around a cylinder or cone, as in a corkscrew or spiral staircase.

Helenium   An American plant of the daisy family which bears many red to yellow flowers, each having a prominent central disk.

Helice A device consisting of revolving blades used to drive a ship or aircraft.

Hell-box A receptacle where cast metal sorts are thrown after printing.

Helot A serf in ancient Sparta; the status between a slave and citizen; a serf or slave.

Heme A precursor to hemoglobin that binds oxygen in the bloodstream.

Hemianopia A partial blindness or a loss of sight in half of your visual field.

Hemiplegia Paralysis of one side of the body.

Hephaestus *In Greek mythology,* the god of fire and forging, and the husband of unfaithful Aphrodite.

Heresiarch The founder of a heresy or the leader of a heretical sect.

Herm A pillar of stone with the head of the god, Hermes, and a large erect phallus in ancient Athens; a square stone pillar with a carved head on top (typically Hermes) used in ancient Greece as a boundary marker or signpost.

Hermeneutic Concerning interpretation, especially the Bible or literary texts.

Hermes The Greek god of commerce, eloquence, invention, travel, and theft who serves as a herald and messenger of the other gods; cf. mercury.

Hermetic Society   Teaches that God is both the all and the creator of the all.

Hermetic   A complete and airtight seal or closure; insulated or protected from outside influences; relating to an ancient occult tradition encompassing alchemy, astrology and theosophy.

Hermetica   Egyptian Greek wisdom texts from the 2nd century, presented as dialogue in which the teacher, Hermes, enlightens a disciple.

Heroick   Obsolete term for heroic.

Hessian   German soldiers who served as auxiliaries to the British Army during the American Revolutionary War.

Hesychasts   The mystical tradition of contemplative prayer in the Eastern Orthodox Church
Heterocatalytic.

Heterocatalytic   *In chemistry*, relating to a catalyst or that which facilitates chemical reaction or change; autocatalytic, catalysis.

Heterocosm   A separate or alternative world.

Heteroecism   The development of different stages of a parasite species on different host plants.

Heterosis   The tendency of a crossbreed individual to show qualities superior to those of both parents.

Hetman   A Polish or Cossack military commander.

Heuretes   To attribute great works of the past to definite persons without much regard to probability.

Hezekiah   The king of Judah under whom the kingdom underwent a ruinous Assyrian invasion at the end of the eighth century B.C.

Hidalgo   *In Spain,* a gentleman.

Hierophant   A person, especially a priest in ancient Greece, who interprets sacred mysteries or esoteric principles.

Hie   To go quickly.

High Church   *In Anglican Christianity*, those who emphasize ritual, often Anglo-Catholic, initially a pejorative term; cf. Low Church.

High feather   To be in high spirits, cheerful.

Highball   A railroad signal to proceed; to travel fast; a drink consisting of whiskey and a mixer such as ginger ale served with ice in a tall glass.

High-binder   A ruffian, especially one of a gang; a swindler, especially a corrupt politician.

Hind   Situated at the back or posterior, especially of a body part.

Hipped   Having hips of a special kind.

Hippo centaur   *In Greek mythology*, a creature with the upper body of a human and lower body of a horse.

Hippogriff A mythical creature with the body of a horse and the wings and head of an eagle, born of the union of a male griffin and a filly.

Hirsute Hairy.

Hirsutism Excessive growth on unexpected areas of the body such as the face, chest, and back.

Hitherto Up until now, or until the point in time under discussion.

Hoarding A billboard.

Hoarfrost A grayish-white crystalline deposit of frozen water vapor formed in clear still weather on vegetation and fences; cf. rime.

Hob A machine tool used for cutting gears or screw threads.

Hocking To life or pull abruptly or with effort.

Hocussed To trick or hoax; to deceive; to befuddle often with drugs; to dope or drug before a race.

Hod A builder's V-shaped open trough on a pole used for carrying bricks and other building material; a coal scuttle.

Hoecake A coarse cake made of cornmeal, originally baked on the blade of a hoe.

Hog-wallow A depression in land made by the wallowing of swine.

Hoi polloi The many.

Hoick   To lift or pull abruptly or with effort; an abrupt pull.

Hoisin   A sweet, spicy, dark red Chinese sauce made from soybeans, vinegar, sugar, and garlic.

Hokum   Nonsense; trite, sentimental, or unrealistic situations, and dialogue.

Holland   A smooth, durable linen fabric used for window shades and furniture covering.

Hollerith   A machine for tabulating and sorting punched cards and tabulating data from them.

Holystoning   The former process of using a soft and brittle sandstone to scrub and whiten wooden decks of ships.

Homburg   A man's felt hat, having a narrow-curled brim and a tapered crown with a lengthwise indentation.

Homely   Lacking in physical attractiveness, not beautiful, unattractive.

Hominy   A coarsely ground corn used to make grits.

Homoeopathic   The treatment of disease by minute doses of natural substances that in a healthy person would produce symptoms of disease; cf. allopathic.

Homology   The state of having the same or similar relation, relative position, or structure.

Honeyfogle   To swindle or dupe; to intend to cheat or trick.

Honoris causa   An honorary degree, a mark of esteem, especially without examination.

Hooch   Alcoholic liquor, especially inferior or illicit whiskey.

Hoodoo   A column or pinnacle of weathered rock; to be bewitched.

Hook   *In land surveying*, a method of indicating the existence of contiguous parcels with the same ownership, the symbol on a map connecting parcel A to parcel B is called the "land hook."

Hoosegow   A prison.

Hop-pillow   A pillow stuffed with hops placed under a sleep pillow believed to induce sleep.

Horatian   Relating to the Roman poet Horace or his work.

Horological   The measurement of time and making of clocks.

Horology   The study and measurement of time; the art of making clocks and watches.

Hors de combat   Out of action due to injury or damage.

Hortatory   To urge to some course of conduct or action; exhorting; encouraging.

Hosanna   To express adoration, praise or joy.

Hot-box   To smoke a cigarette vigorously and rapidly.

Hove Past tense of 'to heave.'

Howdah A seat or pavilion, generally covered, fastened on the back of an elephant for riders.

Hoyden A boisterous girl.

Hudibrastic A kind of comic narrative poetry with jangled rhyming created by Samuel Butler derided the Puritans.

Hugger-mugger To act in a secretive manner.

Hurdy-gurdy A musical instrument with a droning sound played by turning a handle which is attached to a wheel sounding a series of strings with keys worked by the left hand.

Hurley Referring to the stick used in hurling or the game of hurling.

Hurtle To move rapidly or forcefully.

Huysman, Joris Karl, a 19th-century French novelist of the Decadent school.

Hyaline Transparent and usually homogenous.

Hydrocephalus Fluid accumulation in the brain, typically in young children, enlarging the head and sometimes causing brain damage.

Hygeia The goddess of health.

Hymeneal Of or concerning marriage.

Hyperborean   An inhabitant of the extreme north; relating to extreme north; *in Greek mythology,* a member of a race that worshiped Apollo while living in a land of sunshine and plenty beyond the north wind; cf. borean.

Hyperesthesia   Excessive physical sensitivity, especially of the skin.

Hyper   Over; beyond; above; cf. hypo.

Hypertrophy   A nontumorous enlargement of an organ or tissue; to grow or cause to grow abnormally large.

Hypnerotomachia   A book that relates a story of a dream of Poliphilo in which it is shown that all things are a dream and many other things are worthy of knowledge and memory, literally translated the "strife of love in a dream."

Hypolydian   *In music,* an ancient Greek a mode represented on the white keys of the piano by a descending diatonic scale from F to F,

Hypo   Under; below normal; cf. hyper.

Hyraxes   A small, herbivorous mammal with a compact body and very short tail found in arid countries in Africa and Arabia.

Hyssop   A small, bushy aromatic plant of the mint family; *biblically,* a shrub whose twigs were used for Jewish rites of purification.

I

I   When the person speaking is doing the action (I write the songs); cf. me.

Iachimo   A Roman lord and Shakespearean character who is sly and tricky and who wagers over Imogene's chastity.

Iamb   A metrical foot consisting of one short syllable followed by one long syllable; cf. trochee.

Iarbas   *In Roman mythology*, a character who fell in love with the Carthaginian queen Dido who rejected his advances in preference for another suitor.

Ices   Plural for ice; to decorate with icing (like a cake).

Ichthyosauri   An extinct marine reptile of the Mesozoic era resembling a dolphin with a long-pointed head, four flippers and vertical tail.

Ideasthesia   A neuropsychological phenomenon in which activations of concepts evoke perception-like sensory experiences.

Idée fixe   An idea that dominates one's mind, especially for a prolonged period; an obsession.

Idées-recues   A generally accepted concept or idea.

Idely   Lazy, indolent.

Idem sonans   Two names with the same or similar pronunciation or sound; the legal doctrine where a person's identity is presumed known despite the misspelling of his or her name.

Ideograph   A graphic symbol that represents an idea or concept, independent of language, also called an ideogram.

Idiom   A phrase or expression that typically presents a figurative, non-literal meaning, such as *he bit off more than he can chew.*

Idiophone   A musical instrument that vibrates to produce a sound when struck, such as a bell, gong, or rattle.

Idyll   A short description in verse or prose of a picturesque scene or incident, especially in rustic life, that is lighthearted and carefree; extremely happy, peaceful, or picturesque episode or scene, often rustic, and typically idealized; cf. epic.

Il gran refiuto   The grand refusal, the error attributed by the poet Dante to one of the souls he found trapped aimlessly in the Vestibule of Hell.

Illecebrous   To be attractive.

Illicit   Forbidden by laws, rules, or custom; cf. Elicit.

Illume   To light up, illuminate.

Illuminati   People claiming to possess special enlightenment or knowledge of something.

Imagist A poetry movement in the early 20th century in England and America which sought clarity of expression through the use of precise images advanced by Ezra Pound and James Joyce.

Immigrate To come to live permanently in a foreign country; cf. emigrate.

Immure To enclose or confine against one's will, like a prisoner.

Impedimenta Equipment for an activity or expedition, especially when bulky or an encumbrance.

Impend An event about to happen, especially if threatening or significant.

Impended Past tense of impend, or something about to happen.

Imperial A small, pointed beard growing below the lower lip (associated with Napoleon III of France).

Importune To persistently harass someone to do something.

Impresario A person who organizes and often finances concerts, plays, or operas.

Imprimatur A declaration authorizing publication of a book; any mark of approval or endorsement.

In actu *Latin* meaning in the very act; in reality.

In camera *In law*, in private.

In conceptu   Relating to or based on mental concepts; cf. in re.

In esse   *Latin,* meaning in being; in actuality; in actual existence; cf. in posse.

In extremis   An extremely difficult situation; at the point of death.

In flagrante delicto   In legal terms, caught in the very act of wrongdoing, especially an act of sexual misconduct.

In medias res   Into the middle of a narrative; without preamble; into the midst of things.

In partibus infidelium   In the regions of the infidels.

In posse   *Latin*, meaning not in actuality; having a potential to exist; cf. in esse.

In potestate   One having power or authority.

In propria persona   Latin for one's self; in law a person who represents themselves without a lawyer.

In quo warranto   A writ or legal action requiring a person to show by what warrant an office or franchise is held, claimed or exercised.

In re   In the legal case of, with regard to; cf. in conceptu.

In situ   *Latin*, meaning on site or in position, such as in a place to describe where an event takes place and is used in many different contexts.

In status pupillari   In English universities of junior status and under guardianship; not having a master's degree.

In vacuo   In a vacuum; away from or without the normal context or environment.

In your cups   To be drunk.

Inachos   *In Greek mythology*, the first king of Argos after whom a river in Greece is called the Inachus River.

Inamorato   A person's female lover.

Incantate   To influence by magic; to charm, enchant, or bewitch.

Incubus   A male demon believed to have sexual intercourse with sleeping women; a cause of distress or anxiety; a nightmare; cf. Succubi.

Incunabulum or **Incunable**, an early printed book, especially one printed before 1501.

Indefatigable   To persist tirelessly; incapable of being fatigued.

Indigo   A tropical plant of the pea family formerly used as a source of dark blue dye; a color between blue and violet on the spectrum.

Indubitable   Impossible to doubt; unquestionable.

Induration   When the soft tissue of different parts of the body, especially the skin, becomes thicker and harder due to inflammation.

Inflectional A change in the form of a word to express a grammatical function or attribute; the modulation or intonation or pitch in the voice.

Infra dig Beneath one, demeaning.

Infract To break the terms of an agreement.

Infundibulate A funnel-shaped cavity or structure; shaped like a funnel.

Ingenious Clever, original and inventive; cf. disingenuous.

Ingenue An innocent or unsophisticated young woman, especially in a play or film.

Inimical Hostile; harmful.

Inimitable So good or unusual as to be impossible to copy; unique.

Inordinate Unusually or disproportionately large; excessive.

Insensate Lacking physical sensation.

Inspirit To encourage and enliven.

Insufferable Extremely unpleasant or annoying; e.g. insufferable insolence.

Intaglio A design incised or engraved into a material.

Intarsia A method of knitting with a number of colors where a ball of yarn is used for each area of color; an elaborate marquetry using inlays in wood, especially practiced in 15th-century Italy.

Intemptata Latin for untried.

Intensives An intensifier; increasing intensity.

Inter alia Among other things.

Inter arma silent leges Latin for *among arms, the laws are silent* or in times of war, the law falls silent.

Intercalary A day or month inserted in a calendar to harmonize it with the solar year, e. g. February 20 in leap years.

Interconvertible Not open to question, indisputable.

Intercural Between the legs.

Interlineation A legal term for an agreed-upon sentence inserted between lines in a contract that has been typed and signed.

Intern A student or trainee who works, sometimes without pay, at a trade or occupation to gain work experience; cf. extern.

Interrobang The combination of an exclamation mark with a question mark (!?).

Interrogatory Conveying the force of a question; questioning; in law, a written question which must be answered.

Interstice An intervening space, especially a very small one.

Interstitial Occurring in or being an interval or intervening space or segment.

Intone To say or recite with little rise and fall of the pitch of the voice.

Intubate To insert a tube into something, especially the trachea for ventilation.

Inure To accustom someone to something, especially something unpleasant; in law, to come into operation, to take effect.

Inverness cape A water-repellent overcoat with an extra layer of cloth over the shoulders to hinder rain from soaking through.

Invicta *Latin*, meaning invincible, undefeated or unconquered.

Involution The shrinkage of an organ in old age or when inactive.

Io *In Greek mythology*, a maiden seduced by Zeus; an unmarried girl, especially a virgin.

Ione *In Greek mythology*, a sea nymph.

Iota   An extremely small amount; the ninth letter of the Greek alphabet (I or i).

Ipse dixit   An assertion without proof, or dogmatic expression of opinion.

Iritis   Inflammation of the iris of the eye.

Irredentism   A policy of advocating the restoration to a country of any territory formerly belonging to it.

Irredentist   A person advocating the restoration of territory formerly belonging to it.

Irrefragable   Not able to be refuted or disproved; indisputable.

Irrumatio   The active thrusting of a man's penis into one or more body parts of a partner.

Irruption   The sudden change in the population density of an organism.

Iseult   An Irish princess wed to Mark, King of Cornwall, but in love with his knight Tristan.

Isolde   Princess of Ireland and wife of Mark of Cornwall and the lover, and later wife of Tristan.

Isometric   Having equal dimension; *in physiology,* muscular action in which tension is developed without contraction of the muscle.

Isotropic   Materials whose properties remain the same when tested in different directions.

Issue   The action of supplying or distributing an item for use, sale, or official purposes.

Istrian Peninsula   The largest peninsula in the Adriatic Sea located at the head of the Adriatic between the Gulf of Trieste and the Kvarner Gulf shared by three countries (Croatia, Slovenia and Italy).

Iterative   Involving repetition; expressing repetition of a verbal action; using repetition of a sequence of operations.

Ivesian   Pertaining to American composer Charles Ives (1874-1954) whose music is characterized by dissonance.

J

Jacana A small, tropical wading bird with greatly elongated toes and claws that enable it to walk on floating vegetation.

Jackboot A large, leather military boot reaching to the knee.

Jackdaw A small, gray-headed crow noted for its inquisitiveness.

Jackstraw A game in which a set of straws or thin strips is tossed in a heap with each player in turn trying to remove one at a time without disturbing the rest.

Jacobin A member of a group advocating egalitarian democracy and engaging in terrorist activities during the French Revolution of 1789; a member of an extremist or radical political group.

Jacquerie A rebellion of local peasants.

Janissary A Turkish soldier.

Janus *In ancient Roman mythology*, the god of beginnings, gates, time, duality, and endings, usually depicted with two faces looking to the future and past.

Japalac A combination of varnish and stain that revives old woodwork furniture.

Jardinière An ornamental pot or stand for displaying growing plants; a garnish of mixed vegetables.

Jargogle To confuse.

Jarvey *In Ireland,* the driver of a hackney coach or a jaunting car; a hackney coach.

Jehu The driver of a coach or cab; a reckless driver.

Jennet A kind of small Spanish horse; a female donkey.

Jeremiad A long, mournful complaint or lamentation; a list of woes.

Jeremiah A major Hebrew prophet of the sixth and seventh centuries; a person who is pessimistic about the present and foresees a calamitous future.

Jerked Meat that is salted, cut into strips, and dried in the sun.

Jerkin A sleeveless jacket.

Jerkwater Small, remote, and insignificant rural settlements.

Jeunesse dorée A fashionable, wealthy young couple.

Jib To refuse to proceed further; to balk.

Jiggery-pokery Deceitful or dishonest behavior.

Jine To conquer.

Jobbery The practice of using public office or position of trust for one's own gain or advantage.

Jogtrot A slow trot.

Jointure A legal marriage settlement.

Jomini, Baron Antoine Henri A French-Swiss officer, who served as a general in the French and later Russian services, is one of the most celebrated writers on the Napoleonic art of war.

Jonquil A widely cultivated narcissus with clusters of small fragrant yellow flowers native to southern Europe.

Jordan A river in Palestine that empties into the Black Sea; *in Hebrew,* to descend or flow down.

Jouissance Physical or intellectual pleasure, delight or ecstasy.

Joule A unit of energy; cf. exajoule.

Juba A dance originating among plantation slaves in the southern US featuring rhythmic handclapping and slapping of the thighs.

Judder Rapid and forceful shaking and vibration.

Jujube The edible, berry-like fruit of a Eurasian plant; a fruit-flavored gumdrop or lozenge.

Jumper   A tunic.

Jute   A member of a Germanic people from Jutland who invaded Britain in the 5th century.

K

Kale A hardy cabbage that produces erect stems with large leaves and no head.

Kasserine Pass A two-mile-wide gap in the Grand Dorsal Chain of the Atlas Mountains in central Tunisia where, in February 1943, a famous battle took place.

Katydid A large, typically green long-horned grasshopper native to North America.

Kedge To move a ship or boat by hauling in a hawser attached to an anchor dropped at some distance; cf. hawser.

Keening Wailing in grief for a dead person; a prolonged high-pitched sound, typically to express grief or sorrow.

Keep Food, clothes, and other essentials for living; archaic for to be in charge, in control.

Keffiyeh An Arab's kerchief worn as a headdress.

Kenal A long, narrow boat used on canals.

Kenech To laugh loudly.

Kepis A French military cap with a flat top and horizontal brim.

Kerb A rim.

Kerfuffle A commotion or fuss, especially one caused by conflicting views.

Kern A light-armed Irish foot solider; a peasant; a rustic.

Khawal A prostitute.

Khedive The title of the viceroy of Egypt under Turkish rule.

Kibosh To decisively end or reject something.

Kike Pejorative word for a Jew.

Kine Cows collectively.

Kinematograph Obsolete term for a combined camera, printer, and projector; to take a picture with a kinematograph.

Kino Schule A term for new, intimate German films in the 21st century.

Kirtle A woman's gown or outer petticoat, a man's tunic or coat.

Kiver A shallow vessel or wooden tub.

Klezmer Instrumental Jewish music that includes dance, melodies, and improvisation played at social functions.

Knacker To tire someone out; to damage something severely.

Knell The sound of a bell, especially when rung solemnly for a death or funeral.

Kohl An antimony sulfide black powder used as eye makeup, especially in Eastern countries.

Kongoni A hartebeest (animal), usually pale-yellow or brown found in Kenya and Tanzania.

Kossuth A hat with a flat-topped crown and rolled brim.

Krater A large vase in ancient Greece used for the dilution of wine with water; a bell shape turned upside down, as in a vase.

Krupke A police sergeant named after a character in *West Side Story.*

Kufi A brimless, short, round cap worn by men in Africa commonly called a topi or tupi.

Kvass A fermented drink low in alcohol made from rye flour with malt.

Kylix An ancient Greek cup with a shallow bowl and a tall stem.

L

L'homme mayen sensual   A man of average appetites.

La belle nature   Beautiful nature, beautiful natural surroundings.

Laager   An entrenched position that is defended against opponents; a camp or encampment formed by a circle of wagons.

Là   bas   French for over there, there, yonder.

Lace   To draw together edges; to draw or pass.

Lacquey   A servile follower, a hanger-on.

Lacrimator   A substance that irritates the eyes and causes tears to flow.

Lagniappe   Something given as a bonus or extra gift.

Laicized   To withdraw clerical status from someone or thing; to secularize.

Lamé   A fabric with interwoven gold or silver threads.

Lampblack   A black pigment made from soot.

Lampion A paper lantern.

Landline *In the military*, telephones connected by a wire.

Landskip Archaic for landscape.

Lanista The director and trainer of a gladiatorial school.

Laocoön A Trojan priest killed by two sea serpents after warning the Trojans against the wooden horse.

Lapidary prose Prose appropriate for memorials, mausoleums, stelae, and other commemorations in which words are etched in stone; concise, pithy, elegant, and sententious.

Lapidary Relating to stone and gems and the work involved in engraving, cutting and polishing; cf. Lapidary prose.

Lappet A decorative flap, fold or hanging part of a headdress or garment.

Laputa An imaginary flying island in Swift's *Gulliver's Travels* where the inhabitants engage in a variety of ridiculous projects.

Lapwing A large plover bird with a black and white head and underparts, and a loud call; cf. peewit.

Lariat To secure with a lariat fastened to a stake, as a horse or mule for grazing; to lasso or catch with a lariat.

Lar *In ancient Rome,* the guardian god of the household.

Lateen A triangular sail on a long yard at an angle of 45 degrees to the mast.

Latibulate To hide in an attempt to escape reality.

Latitudinarian Allowing latitude in religion; showing no preferences among varying creeds and forms of worship.

Laudanum An alcoholic solution containing morphine prepared from opium and formerly used as a narcotic painkiller.

Launisch To be peevish.

Laved To wash, like with water, against or over something.

Lavender A small, aromatic evergreen shrub of the mint family with bluish-purple flowers used in perfumery and medicine in ancient times; the characteristics of refinement and gentility; a pale blue color with a trace of mauve.

Lave To wash, e. g. to lave your face.

Lazarus The biblical story of Lazarus who was poor, homeless, and a beggar and goes to heaven at his death while the rich man goes to hell.

Leadpipe In a brass instrument, the pipe or tube into which the mouthpiece is placed.

Leads *In Britain*, a leash for a dog or other animal.

Lector A reader, especially someone who reads lessons in a church service.

Lecythos A large South American tree distinguished by a woody, operculate capsular fruit.

Ledgermain The skillful use of one's hands when performing conjuring tricks; legerdepied.

Leech The aft or back edge of a fore and aft sail; cf. gore, goring.

Leek A plant related to the onion with flat, overlapping leaves forming an elongated cylindrical bulb eaten as a vegetable; the Welsh national emblem.

Legerdepied Sleight of foot; cf. ledgermain.

Leman A lover or sweetheart; an illicit lover, especially a mistress.

Lenten Pertaining to Lent.

Lentigines Sun spots.

Leonine Of or resembling a lion.

Lerna A city and fountain in a swampy region south of Argos, known for the quality of its water.

Les Paradis Artificiels A book by Charles Baudelaire about being under the influence of opium and hashish describing their effects and ways in which they could be used to aid mankind in reaching an ideal world.

Lèse majesté Insulting a monarch or other ruler; treason.

Lest   The intention of preventing something, usually undesirable; to avoid the risk of.

Lettrine   An initial or drop cap letter at the beginning of a writing piece; the initial letter.

Leucocytosis   An excess of white blood corpuscles.

Levant   The historical area consisting of the Eastern Mediterranean region of Western Asia; a runaway, typically leaving unpaid debts; cf. Levantine.

Levantine   Relating to a Levant; cf. Levant.

Levée   An embankment built to prevent the overflow of a river.

Levered   An equity that has be leveraged using debt.

Lexis   The total stock of words in a language.

Liana   A woody climbing plant/vine that hangs from trees, especially in tropical rainforests.

Liaotung Peninsula   A peninsula in northeast China just west of North Korea.

Liber Vagatgorum   A book also known as The Book of Vagabonds and Beggars with a vocabulary of their language attributed to Martin Luther.

Libertad   Freedom.

Librettist   A person who writes the text of an opera or other long vocal work.

Libretto   The text of an opera or other long vocal work.

Lickspittle   A person who behaves obsequiously to those in power.

Liffey   The River Liffey is a river in Ireland that flows through the centre of Dublin.

Lignite   A soft, brownish coal with traces of plant structure, intermediate between bituminous coal and peat.

Lilt   A characteristic rising and falling of the voice when speaking; a pleasant gentle accent; cf. lilting.

Lilting   To speak, sing, or sound with a lilt; cf. lilt.

Limber   A two-wheeled cart used to support the trail of an artillery piece allowing it to be towed: to warm up in preparation for exercise or activity, especially sports.

Limbic   A group of subcortical structures (hypothalamus, hippocampus, and amygdala) of the brain that are concerned with emotion and motivation.

Limey   Pejorative word for an Englishman.

Limpet   A marine mollusk with a shallow conical shell and broad muscular foot that is usually found clinging to rocks.

Lineament   A distinctive characteristic, especially of the face; in geology, a linear feature on the earth's surface such as a fault.

Lingua franca A language that is adopted as a common language between speakers whose native languages are different; historically, a mixture of Italian with French, Greek, Arabic and Spanish formerly used in the Levant.

Lingual Relating to or near or on the side toward the tongue.

Linn A waterfall; the pool below a waterfall; a steep precipice.

Linnaean Characteristic of the Swedish botanist Carolus Linnaeus and his modern system of botany and zoology.

Lintel A horizontal support of timber, stone, concrete or steel across the top of a door or window.

Lion-painter The Lion Painter is an Athenian black-figure painter active ca. 630-600 BC.

Liquorish Lecherous, lustful; greedy, longing.

Lithography A method of printing from a flat surface where unnecessary ink is turned away from the surface, usually by grease.

Littérateur A person who is interested in and knowledgeable about literature.

Littoral Relating to or situated on the shore of the sea or a lake; a region lying along a shore.

Liturgical The customary public worship performed by a religious group.

Liveried One who wears a special uniform; cf. livery.

Livery   A special uniform worn by a servant or official; an identifying design, such as a uniform, ornament, symbol or insignia that designates ownership or affiliation, often found on an individual or vehicle; a stable; cf. liveried.

Ljubljana Gap   A strategic mountain pass between the Alps and Dinaric Alps located between Trieste and Ljubljana in Slovenia.

Loam   A fertile soil of clay and sand containing humus.

Locarno   A town in southern Switzerland; in *The Pact of Locarno,* Germany renounced the use of force to change its western frontiers.

Lochia   The sign that a uterus is recovering after childbirth and the normal vaginal discharge from a healing uterus; discharge from the vagina after giving birth.

Locofoco   A member of a radical group of New York Democrats organized in 1835 in opposition to the regular party organization; a friction match developed in the 19th century ignited by rubbing it against any hard surface.

Locum tenens   A person who temporarily fulfills the duties of another, especially with clergy and physicians.

Locus classicus   A passage considered to be the best known or most authoritative on a particular subject.

Lodgment   An enclave taken and defended by force of arms against determined opposition; a place in which a person or thing is located, deposited or lodged.

Loggia   A gallery or room with one or more open sides, especially one that forms a part of a house and has one side open to a garden.

Loggie   A covered area on the side of a building, especially one that serves as a porch; an open balcony in a theater.

Logomachy   An argument without words.

Logothete   A bureaucrat or petty accountant.

Lohengrin   *In Germanic legend*, son of Parsifal and knight of the Holy Grail.

Lollapalooza   A person or thing that is particularly impressive or attractive.

Lombrosianism   Relating to the criminology doctrines of Lombroso and especially that a criminal is a definite physical type and mental stigmata and is the product of heredity, atavism and degeneracy.

Longueurs   A tedious passage in a book or other work.

Loom   An apparatus for making fabric by weaving yarn or thread; to appear as a large shape that is not clear, usually in a threatening way.

Loop Hole   an arrow or slit in a wall.

Lope   To run or move with long bounding strides.

Lordosis   Excessive inward curvature of the spine.

Lorgnon   A monocle or pair of spectacles.

Lothair A famous warrior synonymous with strength, vigor, and masculinity.

Loth Reluctant, unwilling; cf. loathe.

Louche Disreputable or sordid in a rakish or appealing way.

Louvain A city in east Brussels, Belgium, known for its breweries.

Low Church *In Anglican Christianity*, those who give little emphasis to ritual, usually denoting Protestant emphasis; cf. High Church.

Lowering Darkening and threatening; gloomy.

Lowing The characteristic deep sound of cows.

Lown Syndrome A pre-excitation syndrome of the heart characterized by episodes of abnormal heart racing.

Loxias Crooked or slanting; name for mythical god Apollo because he could prophesy.

Lozenge A diamond-shaped shield bearing the arms of a spinster or widow; a rhombus or diamond shape.

Lucre Money, especially when regarded as sordid or distasteful or gained in a dishonorable way.

Lucubration Archaic for intensive study, laborious work or thought, especially at night; writing that is pedantic or over-elaborate.

Lucullan Extremely luxurious, lavish; relating to Lucullus or his lifestyle.

Lugubrious Sad, mournful, dismal, gloomy.

Lumbago Pain in the muscles and joints of the lower back.

Lumber Disused goods.

Lumpen To be uninterested in revolutionary advancement, especially in Marxist contexts.

Lunette A half-moon-shaped architectural space filled with sculpture, painted, glazed, or masonry.

Lunged Having lungs, especially of a specified kind.

Lupercal An ancient Roman festival of purification and fertility.

Lustra A period of five years; in ancient Rome a purificatory sacrifice made after a census every five years.

Lustrate To purify by sacrifice, ceremonial washing or some other action.

Lusus A deviation from the normal; freak.

Lutefisk A Scandinavian dish of dried cod boiled into a gelatinous consistency.

Lyceum A hall for public lectures or discussions.

Lynching-bee A grand party centered on the spectacle of hanging and burning a black person in full view of the crowd.

M

Mabinogion   The earliest Welsh prose stories that belong to the Matter of Britain compiled in the 12th and 13th centuries.

Mackinaw   A short coat or jacket made of thick, heavy woolen cloth typically with a plaid design.

Mackintosh   A full-length, waterproof coat.

Maenad   A female follower of Bacchus associated with divine possession and frenzied rites, literally translated to *raving ones*.

Mafic   Dark-colored materials such as pyroxene and olivine.

Magniloquent   High-flown or bombastic language.

Mahamanvantara   A period of time equal to the lifespan of Brahma or 311,040,000,000,000 years.

Maieutic   Relating to or resembling the Socratic method of eliciting ideas from another.

Maji   A wise man or king.

Majolica   A kind of earthenware made in imitation Italian maiolica, especially in England during the 19th century.

Majo   Nice, lovely or pleasant.

Majus   Persian term meaning Zoroastrian, and especially Zoroastrian priests.

Malachite   A bright-green mineral consisting of copper capable of taking a high polish.

Malagrugrous   Dismal.

Malefic   Causing or capable of causing harm or destruction, especially by supernatural means.

Malgré lui   In spite of himself or herself.

Mana   Pervasive supernatural or magical power.

Mandela   A geometric figure representing the universe in Hindu and Buddhist symbolism; a symbol in a dream representing the dreamer's search for completeness and self-unity.

Mandorla   In medieval art a pointed oval figure enclosing figures such as Jesus Christ or the Virgin Mary.

Mangle   A mechanical laundry wringer consisting of two rollers powered by a hand crank.

Manifold   Many and various.

Manqué   Having failed to become what one might have been, unfulfilled.

Manse A house occupied by a minister of a Presbyterian church, a person's house.

Mantalini From Charles Dickens, a fashionable dressmaker.

Manumission To release from slavery.

Marabout A Muslim holy man or hermit, especially in North Africa.

Marchioness The wife or widow of a marquee.

Mareotic Sea A brackish lake near Alexandria, Egypt.

Marginalia Marginal notes in a book.

Marguerite An oft-cultivated Eurasian daisy that has large white flowers with yellow centers, also known as an oxeye daisy.

Mariolatry Idolatrous worship of the Virgin Mary.

Marlian In Nigerian a hearing person or free thinker.

Marmora Latin for marble.

Marmoreal Made of or likened to marble.

Marquetry Inlaid work made from small pieces of variously colored wood or other materials used chiefly to decorate furniture.

Marquis The five ranks of British nobility are, in ascending order, Duke, Marquis, Earl, Viscount and Baron, the Marquis protected their respective kingdoms frontier lands: cf. Duke, Earl, Viscount and Baron.

Marsyas *In Greek mythology,* a satyr who lost in a flute-playing contest with Apollo and was flayed alive as a penalty.

Massif A compact group of mountains, especially one that is separate from other groups.

Mastic An aromatic gum or resin that exudes from the bark of a Mediterranean tree used in making varnish, chewing gum and flavoring.

Mastiff A dog of a large, strong breed with drooping ears and pendulous lips.

Mastitis Inflammation of the mammary gland in the breast typically due to bacterial infection via damage to the nipple or teat.

Matelot A sailor.

Matlock A town in England on the River Derwent.

Matters of Britain A body of medieval literature and legendary material associated with Great Britain and its legendary kings and heroes, particularly King Arthur.

Mattock An agricultural tool shaped like a pickax with an adze and chisel at the ends of the head; cf. adze.

Matutine Rising in or just before the dawn.

Maudit   Accursed, wretched.

Maunder   To talk in a rambling manner.

Mauve   A pale purple color.

Maya   Illusion; the Hindu belief that humans view life through distorting veils which prevents seeing reality.

Mazuma   Money, cash.

Mazzaltov   A Jewish phrase expressing congratulations or wishing someone good luck.

Mead   An alcoholic drink of fermented honey and water.

Meander   A winding curve or bend of a river or road.

Meat safe   A container or cupboard used for storing meat with a wire or net cover to protect it.

Mechanism   The philosophic view that holds all phenomena are solely determined by mechanical principles, therefore they can be explained by mechanical principles alone.

Medias res   *Latin for* into the heart of the matter; cf. mediis rebus.

Mediatrix   A woman who is a mediator.

Mediis rebus   *Latin for* in the midst of things; cf. medias res.

Medley   A varied mixture of people or things, a miscellany; in music, a piece composed from parts of existing pieces, usually three, played one after another; cf. mélange.

Medway A river in southeast England flowing through Kent and the Medway towns.

Meerschaum A soft, white claylike material consisting of hydrated magnesium silicate found chiefly in Turkey; a tobacco pipe with a bowl made from meerschaum.

Megarithma A symbolic, dark personality.

Megaron The great hall in ancient Greek palace complexes.

Mélange A mixture; a medley; cf. medley.

Meleager *In Greek mythology*, the leader of a hunt for a boar that had ravaged the country and eventually kills it.

Meme An element of culture or system of behavior that is passed from one individual to another by nongenetic means, especially imitation; a humorous image or text that is copied and spread rapidly via the internet.

Memetic Adjective form of meme; cf. meme.

Menhaden A fish of the herring family that occurs along the east coast of North America and whose oil-rich flesh is used to make fish meal and fertilizer.

Mens sana in corpore sano *A healthy mind in a healthy body*, meaning physical exercise is as important as mental and psychological well-being.

Menses Blood and other matter discharged from the uterus.

Mercenary Primarily concerned with making money at the expense of ethics; a professional solider hired to serve in a foreign army.

Mercer A dealer in textile fabrics, especially silks, velvets and other fine materials.

Mercury The Roman god of commerce, eloquence, invention, travel, and theft who serves as a herald and messenger of the other gods cf. Hermes.

Mercutio A fictional character from Shakespeare's *Romeo and Juliet*, a friend to both and capable of mingling in both houses.

Merino A sheep of a breed with long, fine wool; a soft wool and cotton material resembling cashmere.

Mermen The male equivalent of a mermaid.

Mesmerism Also called animal magnetism, from 18th-century German doctor Franz Mesmer who believed an invisible natural force possessed all living things.

Mesmerist A therapeutic system of F.A. Mesmer; hypnotism.

Metaphor A figure of speech in which a word or phrase is applied to an object or action to which it is not literally applicable; cf. simile.

Metathesis The transposition of sounds or letters in a word, such as pronouncing *ask* as *aks*.

Metempsychosis The supposed transmigration of death of the soul of a human being or animal into a new body of the same or different species.

Methuselah A biblical ancestor of Noah reported to have lived 969 years; an oversized wine bottle holding about six liters.

Methylate Mix or impregnate with methanol.

Metic A foreigner living in an ancient Greek city who had some of the privileges of citizenship.

Metonym A word, name or expression used as a substitute for something else which is closely related, e.g., Washington is a metonym for the federal government of the US.

Metonymy A figure of speech in which a thing or concept is referred to by the name of something closely related to it, e. g. in *the pen is mightier than the sword, pen* stands for thought and *sword* for warfare.

Metrican Measuring or measure; musical meter; rhythmic music.

Me When the person speaking is receiving (the song was given to me); cf. I.

Mewl To cry feebly or querulously; to whimper.

Mews A group of stables with rooms above around a yard or long alley; a row of houses built like mews.

Mezzotint   A print from an engraved copper or steel plate on which the surface has been partially roughened for shading and partially scraped smooth giving light areas.

Micawber   Wilkins Micawber is a Charles Dickens' fictional character from *David.*

Mick   Pejorative word for an Irishman.

Microbiome   The aggregate of all microbiota that reside on or in human tissues and biofluids.

Micturate   To urinate.

Micturition   The action of urinating.

Mien   A person's look or manner, especially one of a particular kind indicating their character or mood.

Milch   A cow or other domestic mammal giving or kept for milk.

Mileage   An allowance for traveling expenses at a certain rate per mile.

Milksop   A person who is indecisive and lacks courage.

Milliard-dollar   A few or couple of million dollars.

Millocracy   A rich class of people who own mills.

Mimosa   An Australian acacia tree with delicate fernlike leaves and yellow flowers; a cocktail composed of champagne and chilled citrus juice, usually orange juice.

Mince To cut up or grind food into very small pieces; to walk with an affected delicacy or fastidiousness, typically with short quick steps.

Minerva The Roman goddess of wisdom, medicine, commerce, handicrafts, poetry, and the arts in general.

Minimus The small toe or finger.

Ministration The provision of assistance or care.

Minnaloushe A free spirit always seeking change, adventure, and excitement.

Minute *Latin for* small, as in a minute message.

Minx An imprudent, cunning, or boldly flirtatious girl or young woman.

Miry Very muddy or boggy.

Misbecome To be unsuitable, unbecoming, or unfit.

Miscible *Of liquids*, forming a homogenous mixture when added together.

Mise en scène The arrangement of the scenery and stage properties in a play.

Missal A book containing the texts used in Catholic Mass throughout the year.

Mite A minute arachnid with four pairs of legs related to tics that live in the soil and are sometimes parasitic on plants and animals.

Miter   A tall headdress worn by bishops as a symbol of office, tapering to a point at the front and back with a deep cleft between; a joint made between two pieces of wood at a 90-degree angle such that the line of junction bisects this angle; cf. mitred.

Mitred   To make a miter; cf. miter.

Mixologist   A bartender.

Mixolydian   In music and other venues, the mode for sentiment and passion, often used by Sappho, an archaic Greek poet from Lesbos known for her lyric poetry and regarded as one of the greatest lyric poets.

Mizzen   On a sailing ship, the mast aft of the ship's main mast.

Mnemonic   A memory device or technique that aids information retention or retrieval in human memory.

Modus Vivendi   Latin for "mode of living" or "way of life" often used to mean an arrangement or agreement that allows conflicting parties to coexist in peace.

Mohist   An ancient Chinese philosophy of ethics and logic from Mozi that advocated a unified ethical and political order emphasizing concern for all, opposition to military aggression, and devotion to frugality and condemnation of waste and luxury.

Moiety   One of two equal parts; half.

Moil   To work hard; drudgery.

Moira   Greek for individual destiny, fate.

Mole   A massive work formed of masonry and large stones or earth laid in the sea as a pier or breakwater; a spy who achieves over a long period an important position within the security defenses of a country.

Moll   A gangster's female companion; a prostitute.

Moloch   A harmless spiny lizard with grotesque appearance that feeds on ants found in inland Australia.

Monocularly   Involving or affecting a single eye.

Monologisum   A soliloquy.

Monologium   Latin for existence is derived from.

Monongahela   A river in central West Virginia and southwestern Pennsylvania known locally as the Mon.

Monopole   A single eclectic charge or magnetic pole; a radio antenna or pylon consisting of a single pole or rod.

Monopolist   A person or business that has a monopoly.

Monsignori   An honorific form of address or title for certain male clergy members.

Monsterful   Wonderful.

Montage   The process or technique of selecting, editing and piecing together separate sections of film to form a continuous whole.

Montagnard A member of hill-dwelling people in Southeast Asia, especially those in the highlands of Vietnam.

Moon To behave or move in a listless and aimless manner.

Moor *In Britain*, a tract of open uncultivated upland; a heath; cf. wold, heath.

Moot Subject to debate, dispute, or uncertainty; having little or no relevance.

Moraine A mass of rocks and sediment carried down and deposited by a glacier typically as ridges at its edges.

Morbidezza The effect of extreme softness and delicacy in pictorial and sculptural representations.

Moreen A bed with a curtain.

Morpheme A meaningful morphological unit of a language that cannot be further divided; cf. etymon, morphological.

Morphological In linguistics, relating to the forms of words; cf. etymon, morpheme.

Morrow The following day; the time following an event; the near future.

Mossback An old-fashioned or extremely conservative person.

Mot juste The exact, appropriate word.

Mote A tiny piece of substance.

Motoric Relating to muscular movement.

Mouchoir A handkerchief.

Mountebank A person who deceives others, especially to get their money; a charlatan.

Movere *In Latin,* to move; considered one of the primary forces that activates or energizes behavior.

Muckrake A person who searches for and tries to expose corruption, scandal, and wrongdoing, especially in politics.

Mud-digger A laborer who digs ditches.

Mud-lighter An open, flat-bottomed boat operated by a mud-digger.

Muezzin A man who calls Muslims to prayer from the minaret of a mosque.

Mufti A Muslim legal expert who is empowered to give rulings on religious matters; plain or ordinary clothes.

Mugwump A person who remains aloof or independent, especially from party politics.

Mull A rounded hill, a summit, and a mountain that is devoid of trees.

Mullein An herbaceous plant with wooly leaves and tall spikes of yellow flowers native to Eurasia.

Mullet A marine fish that is widely caught for food.

Mullion   A vertical bar between the panes of glass in a window.

Multeity   Manifoldness; multiplicity; the quality of being many.

Mummery   A ridiculous, hypocritical, or pretentious ceremony or performance.

Muscadine   Any group of wine grapes native to Mexico and the southeastern USA, typically having thick skins and a musky flavor.

Muscatel   A grape, especially grown for drying to make raisins.

Museal   Pertaining to a museum, or more specifically, museum storage or exhibition.

Muslin   A hemmed, square, white lightweight cotton cloth used to wipe up regurgitated milk when feeding a burping baby.

Musquin   A name meaning honesty, sacrifice and admiration.

Muss-a-row   Obsolete for a game in which players scramble for small objects thrown on the ground.

Mustachio   A long or elaborate mustache.

Mutatis mutandis   *Latin for* with the necessary changes, indicating that while it may be necessary to make some changes to take account of different situations, the main point remains the same.

Myoglobin   A red protein containing heme which carries and stores oxygen in muscle cells; cf. heme.

Myrmidon   *In Greek mythology,* an ancient Thessalian Greek tribe; a follower or subordinate of a powerful person, typically one who is unscrupulous or carries out orders unquestioningly.

Myrrh   A fragrant gum resin obtained from certain trees used in perfumery, medicine, and incense.

Mystogogue   A teacher or propounder of mystical doctrines.

Mythopoeia   The making of a myth or myths.

N

N. G. No good; it doesn't matter, it's not important.

Naggin *In Ireland,* a 200 ml bottle of spirits.

Nankeen A yellowish cotton cloth; the characteristic yellowish buff color of nankeen.

Nape The back of a person's neck.

Nap Fibers on the surface of a cloth.

Naphtha A flammable liquid hydrocarbon mixture.

Natura naturans What is in itself and is conceived through itself, or substance and its attributes, and not another entity, that express an infinite and eternal essence.

Nature *From Latin,* birth.

Nave The central part of a church building that accommodates the congregation; cf. chancel.

Ne plus ultra The perfect or most extreme example of its kind; the ultimate.

Neapolitan   A native or citizen of Naples; an ice cream, sometimes called Harlequin ice cream, composed of three separate flavors arranged side by side.

Neck stock   A made-up, stiffly arranged cravat worn in the 18th century.

Neckcloth   A large, folded ornamental cloth formerly worn loosely around the neck by men; archaic for necktie.

Necromancer   A practice of magic involving communication with the dead; a magician.

Necropolis   A cemetery; cf. acropolis.

Née   Originally called (Ann Newlands married Gary Johnson and became Ann Johnson, née Newlands); born.

Negus   A ruler or the supreme ruler of Ethiopia; sweetened wine.

Nemesis   The Greek goddess of vengeance; the inescapable agent of someone's downfall; a long-standing rival.

Neolin   One of several Delaware prophets whose name means *the enlightened*, in the latter part of the 18th century.

Neologism   A newly coined word or expression.

Neonate   A newborn child.

Neoteny   The delaying or slowing of the physiological development of an organism, typically an animal, also called juvenilization; the retention of juvenile features in the adult animal.

Nepenthe A drug described in Homer's Odyssey that banishes grief or trouble from a person's mind; a plant of the pitcher plant genus.

Nereid A bristle worm of the polychaete family.

Nerts Denial of disparagement.

Nettle A herbaceous plant with jagged leaves covered with stinging hairs; archaic to beat or sting someone with nettles.

Neuropathy Disease or dysfunction of peripheral nerves typically causing numbness or weakness.

Nib The pointed end part of a pen which distributes the ink on a writing surface.

Nidiform Nest shaped.

Nigh Almost; a short distance away.

Nil desperandum Do not despair; never despair.

Nimbus A luminous vapor, cloud, or atmosphere about a god.

Nippy Rather cold, chilly; quick, nimble.

Nisi *In law*, a decree, order or rule taking effect or having validity only after certain conditions are met.

Nisus A mental or physical effort to attain an end; a perfective urge or endeavor.

Nodding To fall asleep or doze, especially while sitting.

Noetic Relating to mental activity or the intellect.

Nolo episcopari *Latin for* I do not wish to be bishoped, a traditional refusal by a Roman Catholic cleric to refuse the offer to be a bishop.

Nome One of the thirty-six territorial divisions of ancient Egypt; an administrative division in modern Greece.

Non plus ultra *Latin for* no more beyond.

Non sequitur A conclusion or statement that does not logically follow from the previous argument or statement.

Nonce A word or expression coined for one occasion; a person who commits a crime involving sex, especially sex with a child.

Nonplussed Bewildered, unsure, bothered, fazed, vexed; cf. plussed.

Nosegay A small bunch of flowers, typically sweet-scented.

Nota bene Observe carefully or take special notice (often used in written text to draw attention to what follows).

Nother Another, entirely different, a whole other.

Notion A vague or imperfect idea or general understanding of something.

Notwithstanding In spite of, in spite of the fact that, nevertheless .

Novella   A narrative prose fiction whose length is shorter than most novels but longer than most short stories.

Nubbin   A small lump or residual part.

Nuc Dimittis   The Song of Simeon used as a canticle in Christian liturgy, especially a compline and evensong; cf. compline, evensong.

Nugatory   Of no value or importance.

Nuggety   A stocky or thickset person.

Nullity   A thing of no importance or worth; in law, the state of being legally void; invalidity.

Numen   The spirit or divine power presiding over a thing or place, "the spirit of the place" or numen.

Numerosity   A large number, especially of people.

Numismatic   Relating to or consisting of coins, paper currency, and medals.

Nunc dimittis   Known as the Song of Simeon, used as a canticle in Christian liturgy, especially at compline and evensong, whose opening line is *Lord, now lettest thou they servant depart in peace.*

Nuncheon   A drink or light snack taken in the afternoon; refreshment between meals.

Nunevite   An inhabitant of the ancient Assyrian city of Nineveh.

O

Oakum Loose fiber obtained by untwisting old rope, used especially in caulking wooden ships.

Objurgate To rebuke severely, to scold.

Obsequious Obedient or attentive to an excessive or servile degree.

Obtrude To become noticeable in an unwelcome or intrusive way.

Obverse The opposite or counterpart of a fact or truth; the side of a coin or medal bearing the head or principal design.

Ocher An earthy pigment containing ferric oxide varying from light yellow to brown or red.

Octavo *Latin for* in eights; the size of a book page that results from folding each printed sheet into eight leaves.

Odalisque A female slave or concubine in a harem.

Odditorium A side-show.

Odist A person who composes odes.

Odsblood God's blood.

Oestrum Female estrus, a recurring period of sexual receptivity and fertility in female mammals; heat.

Oeuvre The works of a painter, composer or author regarded collectively.

Officiant A person, typically a priest or minister, who performs a religious service or ceremony.

Offscour Someone rejected by society, an outcast; something that is scoured off; refuse.

Oinochoe *In ancient Greece and Rome,* a wine pitcher characterized by a handle extending from the lip to the shoulder and a round trefoil mouth.

Okeanos God of the ocean.

Okra A plant of the mallow family with long ridged seedpods eaten as a vegetable and used in soups and stews.

Old tar An old, experienced tailor.

Oleaginous Rich in or producing oil; oily or greasy; exaggerated and distastefully complimentary; obsequious.

Ombré The blending of one hue to another, usually by moving tints and shades from light to dark.

Omne scibile *From Horace,* all the persons of that ilk.

Omnibus A volume containing several novels or other items previously published separately; comprising several items.

Omnigenous Composed of or containing all varieties.

Omphale Queen to whom Hercules was enslaved for a year.

Omphalopsychites One who stares fixedly at their navel to induce a mystical trance.

Omphalos The center or hub of something; *in Greek mythology,* a rounded stone representing the navel of the earth.

Onanism Self-gratification, masturbation; coitus interruptus.

Oneiric Relating to dreams or dreaming.

Onomatological The study of name formation and naming practices.

Onomatopoeic A word that phonetically imitates, resembles, or suggests the sound that it describes, e.g., sizzle.

Ontogenesis The development of an individual organism or anatomical or behavioral feature from the earliest stage to maturity; cf. ontogeny.

Ontogeny The same as ontogenesis; cf. ontogenesis.

Onyx A semiprecious agate with different colors in layers; cf. sardonyx, sard.

Opera hat A collapsible top hat.

Operculate   A hobble or fetter for a horse or other animal.

Opium eater   A person who uses opium as a recreational drug; an opium addict.

Oppugnant   Opposing, antagonistic.

Opus   Any artistic work, especially one on a large scale.

Orangeade   A drink made with orange juice, sweetener, and water, sometimes carbonated.

Oratorio   A large-scale musical work for orchestra and voices, typically with a religious narrative, performed without costumes, scenery or action.

Orbiter dictum   A judge's incidental expression of opinion, not essential to the decision and not establishing precedent; an incidental remark.

Ordinarie   A restaurant.

Ordonnance   The proper or orderly arrangement of parts in such things like painting or literary work.

Ore rotundo   With rounded mouth.

Oread   *In mythology*, a nymph believed to inhabit mountains.

Organicist   The philosophical view that the universe ought to be considered alive and naturally ordered, as a living organism.

Organology   The science of musical instruments and their classifications.

Organon   An instrument of thought, especially a means of reasoning or system of logic, for the acquisition of knowledge.

Oriel   A projection from the wall of a building, typically supported from the ground or by corbels; cf. corbel.

Ormolu   A gilding technique of applying finely ground, high-carat gold mercury amalgam to a bronze object leaving a gold coating.

Ornithopter   A machine designed to achieve flight by means of flapping wings.

Orotund   Something full, round and imposing, like a voice or physique.

Orrery   A clockwork mechanism showing the motions of the planets around the sun.

Orthography   The conventional spelling system of a language.

Orthopterous   Pertaining to the Orthoptera order of insects including cockroaches, crickets, and grasshoppers, characterized by leathery forewings, membranous hind wings and chewing mouthparts.

Oscillography   The study of the wave forms of changing currents in electricity, hence the oscilloscope.

Osculable   That can be kissed.

Oslerize   To euthanize a person because of their old age.

Ostent A significant sign; the act of showing or displaying; appearance, manifestation.

Ostermoor Creative, flexible, studious.

Ostler A groom or stableman employed to take care of horses usually at an inn, also spelled hostler.

Otiose Serving no practical purpose or result; archaic for indolent, idle.

Otologist A doctor who specializes in diseases of the ear; cf. otology.

Otology The science that deals with the ear and its diseases; cf. otologist.

Ouachita A River that rises in western Arkansas and flows southeast into eastern Louisiana to become a tributary of the Red River.

Oubliette A secret dungeon with access only through a trapdoor in its ceiling.

Outré Unusual and startling.

Outscouring That which is scoured out or washed out.

Ouzel Bird that resembles the blackbird.

Overborne Past participle of overborne, overcome by emotional pressure or physical force.

Overmorrow The day after tomorrow.

Oversloughed   To pass over; to pass over for an appointment or promotion in favor of another; to hinder or obstruct.

Oxford   A cardigan sweater is made of wool with buttons, hand pockets, roll sleeve cuffs and woven brixton.

P

P. D. Q. Pretty damned quick.

Packthread A thick thread for sewing or tying up packages.

Paddock A small field or enclosure where horses are kept or exercised.

Padrone An employer, especially one who exploits immigrant workers; *in Italy*, the proprietor of a hotel.

Paeon *In prosody,* a metrical foot of one long syllable and three short syllables in any order.

Palaestra *In ancient Greece and Rome*, a wrestling school or gymnasium.

Palanquin *In India,* A litter carried by porters.

Palate The roof of the mouth; a person's appreciation of taste and flavor, especially when sophisticated and discriminating.

Palatine A high-level official attached to imperial or royal courts in Europe since Roman times; derived from their association with Palatine Hill in ancient Rome; relating to a palace, having sovereign authority.

Palatize   To modify, as the tones of the voice, by means of the palate.

Palaver   Unnecessarily elaborate or complex procedure; a lengthy and unproductive discussion; an improvised conference between two groups, typically those without a shared language or culture.

Pale   A wooden post or strip used as an upright member in a fence; an enclosed barrier, especially made of pales; an area enclosed by a pale.

Palette   A thin board or slab on which an artist lies and mixes colors.

Palfrey   A docile horse used for ordinary riding, especially by women.

Palimpsest   A manuscript or piece of writing material on which the original writing has been erased to make room for the later writing, but of which traces remain.

Paling   A fence made from pointed wooden or metal stakes; cf. pale.

Palinode   A poem in which the poet retracts a view or sentiment expressed in a former poem.

Palisade   A fence of wooden stakes or iron railings fixed in the ground forming an enclosure for defense.

Palmette An ornament of radiating petals that resembles the leaflets of a palm.

Palmetto A fan palm, especially one of a number occurring in the southern US to northern South America.

Palmier A sweet crisp pastry shaped like a palm leaf.

Palmyrian An Asian fan palm tree that yields timber, fiber, and fruit.

Palpate To examine by touch, especially the body for medical purposes.

Palped To touch, feel.

Palsied To be affected by palsy or paralysis and involuntary tremors.

Pandect A complete body of the laws of a country.

Pandied *Mostly British*, to strike the hand with a strap as punishment.

Pang A sudden sharp pain or painful emotion.

Panglossian From Voltaire's *Candide*, the view that all is for the best in this best of all possible worlds; excessively optimistic.

Panjandrum A person who has a great deal of authority or influence.

Pannikin A small, metal drinking cup.

Panopticon A circular prison with cells arranged around a central well from which prisoners can be observed at all times.

Pantalette Long underpants with a frill at the bottom of each leg worn by women and girls in the 19th century.

Panthea *Greek for* of all gods.

Papboat A boat-shaped dish to hold pap for feeding infants or invalids.

Papillae A small, rounded protuberance on a part or organ of the body; a small fleshy projection on a plant.

Paradisiacal Ideal or idyllic; heavenly.

Paralogism A piece of illogical or fallacious reasoning, especially one which appears superficially logical.

Parch To make or become dry through intense heat.

Parfait A dessert consisting of layers of ice cream and fruit served in a tall glass.

Parkinson's Law The principle that public administration, bureaucracy, and officialdom expand regardless of the amount of work to be done; the notion that work expands to fill the time available for its completion, and that deadlines are meaningless.

Parnell, Charles An Irish nationalist politician in the 1980s who advocated Irish home rule.

Parochial Relating to a church or parish; having a limited or narrow outlook or scope.

Parode The first song sung by the chorus as it enters a Greek theater, also called the entrance ode; a side entrance of a theater.

Parodic A parody, a literary or artistic work that uses imitation of an author or work for comic effect and ridicule; something so bad as to be equivalent to intentional mockery, a travesty, e.g., a parody of justice.

Parole The release of someone, like a prisoner, before the completion of their sentence on the promise of good behavior.

Parol Given or expressed orally.

Parquet The front of the ground floor of a theatre.

Parterre A level space in a garden or yard occupied by an ornamental arrangement of flower beds.

Parthenogenesis Reproduction from an ovum without fertilization, especially in some invertebrates and lower plants.

Parthian grin To smirk contemptuously; contempt expressed by mockery in looks or words.

Partialism A sexual interest with a focus on a specific part of the body.

Participle A word formed from a verb and used as an adjective or noun, like *working woman* and *good breeding.*

Particolored   Having two or more different colors.

Partie carrée   A party of four persons.

Parturiate   To bring forth young.

Parturition   The act of giving birth to young; childbirth.

Parvenu   A person of obscure origin who has gained wealth, influence, or celebrity, meant derogatorily.

Pascalian terror   From Blasé Pascal's *Pensées,* the terror of nothingness or infinite space.

Passant   An animal represented as walking with the right front foot raised, usually depicted in profile with the tail raised.

Passata   A thick paste made from strained tomatoes, used especially in Italian cooking.

Passim   *Latin for* throughout or here and there; a word used in footnotes to indicate that a word or subject occurs frequently, e.g., an entry in an index reading "rope 69-90 passim" means that rope is mentioned in pages 69 through 90.

Paté   A person's head.

Patera   A broad shallow dish used in ancient Rome for pouring libations.

Paterfamilias   The male head of a family or household.

Paternoster   The Lord's Prayer, especially in Latin; an elevator consisting of a series of linked, doorless compartments moving continuously on an endless belt.

Pâtés   Liver, meat or fowl finely minced or ground and variously seasoned; pasta.

Pathetic fallacy   The attribution of human feelings and responses to inanimate things or animals, especially in art and literature.

Pathic   A man or boy on whom sodomy is practiced.

Patios   A dialect other than the standard or literary dialect; uneducated or provincial speech.

Patriarchally   Relating to or characteristic of a patriarch; relating to a patriarchal social system.

Patrie   A native country, birthplace, or homeland; fatherland.

Patrimony   Property inherited from one's father or male ancestor.

Patristics   *In theology*, the study of the fathers of the church.

Patronymic   A name derived from the name of a father or male ancestor.

Patter   A song characterized by a fast tempo with rapid succession of rhythmic patterns in which each syllable of text corresponds to one note, common in comic opera and especially Gilbert and Sullivan.

Pavilion A summerhouse or other decorative building used as a shelter in a park or garden; a highly decorated, projecting portion of a building.

Pax atomic A period of severe tensions without a major military conflict.

Peacharino A person or thing that is especially attractive, liked, or enjoyed.

Peart Lively, cheerful.

Peavey A lumberjack's cant hook with a spike at the end; cf. cant.

Peccant To have committed a fault or sin; offending; diseased or causing disease.

Peccavi An acknowledgement of sin.

Peck Food; a quarter of a bushel; a great deal or large or excessive quantity.

Peckish To be hungry.

Peerage Those holding a hereditary or honorary title.

Peewit The northern lapwing; cf. lapwing.

Peg-top Apparel worn over other clothing for warmth.

Peitho *In Greek mythology*, the goddess of persuasion, or winning through eloquence.

Pelisse   A woman's cloak with armholes or sleeves reaching to the ankles.

Pemmican   A food paste of dried pounded meat mixed with melted fat and other ingredients made by North American Indians.

Penetralia   The innermost parts of a building; a secret or hidden place.

Penile   Related to or affecting the penis.

Pennon   A long, triangular flag, especially one attached to a lance or helmet; a pennant.

Pennorth   A penny's worth, or anything that can be bought for a penny; something very small; the least amount.

Pennyroyal Small-leaved plants of the mint family used in herbal medicine.

Penstemon   A North American plant of the figwort family with showy five-lobed flowers, also known as the beardtongue.

Pent   Another term for pent up; cf. unpent.

Pentimento   A visible trace of earlier painting beneath a layer of paint on a canvas.

Penult   A linguistic term for the second to last syllable of a word; archaic term for penultimate.

Peonage A system where an employer compels a worker to pay off a debt with work, also called debt slavery or debt servitude.

Peplos A rich outer robe or shawl worn by women in ancient Greece hanging in loose folds and sometimes drawn over the head.

Pepsis A genus of large, spider-hunting wasps that includes tarantula hawks.

Pepys A change or variation occurring in the course of something.

Per corollary By corollary, a proposition that follows from one already proved.

Per se *Latin for* by or in itself; intrinsically; cf. a se.

Perambulator A baby carriage; a pram; a person who walks, especially for pleasure and in a leisurely way.

Percheron A powerful draft horse of a gray or black breed, originally from France.

Père et fils French for father and son.

Peregrination A journey, especially a long or meandering one.

Perforce By force of circumstances or necessity.

Peri Hypsous Ancient Longinus book meaning *On Height* or *On the Sublime*.

Periactus *In ancient Greek theater,* a revolving prismatic apparatus with a different scene painted on each of three sides.

Perinatal The period of time when you become pregnant and up to a year after giving birth; cf. pre-natal.

Peripety A sudden turn of events or an unexpected reversal, especially in a literary work.

Periphrasis The use of indirect and circumlocutory speech or writing; an indirect and circumlocutory phrase.

Peristaltic The wavelike, involuntary muscular contractions of the digestive tract or other tubular structures by which contents are forced onward toward the opening.

Permittee A person who is given a permit or other official authorization to do something.

Pern mill A mill where weaver's bobbins are manufactured.

Peroration A closing or conclusion.

Persiffled To tease.

Persiflage Light and slightly contemptuous mockery or banter.

Pertinacious Holding firmly to an opinion or a course of action.

Pertinacity The characteristic of being determined to achieve a particular aim.

Pescatarian A person who does not eat meat but does eat fish.

Petit maître Little master.

Petit nègre A small Negro.

Petrichor The way it smells after the rain.

Pet To be in a petulant mood (to be in a pet); to feel or show anger.

Phaeton A light, open, four-wheeled horse-drawn carriage; a vintage touring car.

Phantasmagoria A sequence of real or imaginary images like those seen in a dream.

Phantomatic A phantom; an illusionary perception.

Phillip A male name meaning *lover of horses.*

Philologian The study of literary texts and written records to establish their authenticity and meaning.

Philostratus An ancient Greek sophist philosopher during the Roman imperial period.

Philters A drink that supposedly arouses love and desire for another person, a love potion.

Phiz A person's face or expression.

Phlegm   *In medieval medicine,* one of four bodily humors believed to be associated with a calm, stolid temperament; calmness of temperament.

Phocion   An ancient Athenian statesman made famous by Plutarch who believed extreme frugality was the condition for virtue.

Phosphene   The sheen or light that occurs when the eyes are closed after being pressed by the hands.

Photographic memory   The ability to remember information or visual images in great detail; cf. eidetic.

Phrygian   Relating to Phrygia, a kingdom in antiquity located in west central Anatolia in what is now Turkey.

Phthisic   A wasting disease of the lungs.

Phthisis   Pulmonary tuberculosis or a similar progressive systemic disease.

Phylloxera   A vine louse; cf. prephylloxera.

Phylogenetic   *In biology,* relating to the evolutionary development and diversification of a species or a particular feature of an organism.

Phylogeny   Also known as phylogenesis, the evolutionary development and diversification of a species or group of organisms, or of a particular organism.

Physiognomy   *In art,* the practice of assessing a person's character or personality from their outer appearance, especially the face.

Pianner A measured, assigned or computed numerical quantity.

Pianoforte A formal term for piano.

Picador A bullfighter on horseback who picks the bull with a lance to weaken and goad it .

Pickaninny A small black child; very small.

Piebald Having irregular patches of two colors, typically black and white; an animal having patches of two colors.

Pied à terre A small apartment, house, or room kept for occasional use.

Pied Having two or more colors.

Piedness The quality or state of being pied; variegation; cf. pied, variegation.

Piffle Nonsense.

Pikestaff The wooden shaft of a pike.

Pilaster An ornamental rectangular column, especially one projecting from a wall.

Pilau Rice cooked in seasoned broth with onions or celery and usually poultry, game or shellfish, and sometimes tomatoes.

Pile The raised surface or nap of a fabric, consisting of upright loops or strands of yarn.

Pilfer   To steal, typically things of little value.

Pillion   A woman's light saddle; a cushion attached to the back of a saddle for an additional passenger; a seat for a passenger behind a motorcyclist.

Pillory   A wooden framework with holes for the head and hands in which an offender was imprisoned and exposed to public abuse.

Pinion   The outer part of a bird's wings, including the flight feathers; to tie or hold the arms or legs of someone.

Pink (to)   To perforate in an ornamental pattern.

Pinked   To cut with a scalloped or zigzag edge such as cloth.

Pinole   Sweetened flour made from dried corn mixed with flour made of mesquite beans, sugar, and spices.

Pinon   A small pine tree with edible seeds, native to Mexico and southwestern US.

Pinto   Piebald; a piebald horse; cf. piebald.

Pinxter   A deciduous, pink-flowered azalea.

Pip   A small, hard seed in a fruit; an excellent or very attractive person or thing.

Pipkin   A small earthenware pot or pan.

Pippin   A red and yellow desert apple; an excellent person or thing.

Piquant Having a pleasantly sharp taste or appetizing flavor.

Pique A feeling of irritation or resentment resulting from a slight, especially to one's pride; to stimulate interest or curiosity.

Pirogue A heavy, long and narrow dugout canoe made from a single tree trunk.

Pismire A social insect living in organized colonies.

Pithead The top of a mining pit or coal shaft.

Pithiatric Capable of being cured by persuasion and suggestion.

Pith The important or essential part, the essence, core, or heart of a matter.

Pium A small, black stinging fly from South America.

Place d'armes *In the military*, the parade ground or assembly point for troops and arsenal.

Plainsong A body of chants used in the liturgies or the Western Church.

Plaint *In law*, an accusation or charge; a complaint; a lamentation.

Plaintive Sounding sad and mournful.

Plait A single length of hair made up of three or more interlaced strands, a braid.

Plantain   Bananas in the genus Musa whose fruits are generally used in cooking.

Plasteline   A nonhardening modeling clay made from clay mixed with oil or wax.

Plectrum   A thin piece of plastic held by the fingers, used to pluck the strings of a musical instrument such as a guitar.

Plein air   A 19th-century, outdoor painting style with a strong sense of the open air that became popular in French impressionism; the act of painting outdoors.

Plenary   Unqualified, absolute, sweeping, or comprehensive; a meeting to be attended by all participants at a conference or assembly who otherwise meet in smaller groups.

Pleonasm   The use of more words than are necessary to convey a meaning such as *see with one's eyes* and *a free gift*.

Plethoric   *In medicine*, excessively full of bodily fluid, particularly blood; overly large or abundant; excessive.

Pleura   Serous membranes lining the thorax and enveloping the lungs in humans and other mammals.

Pleurisy   Inflammation of the pleurae, or lung lining, which imparts lubrication, and causes pneumonia.

Pleuropneumonia   Combined inflammation of the pleura and lungs; an acute febrile and often fatal respiratory disorder of cattle, goats, and sheep.

Plosive The sound that occurs when the air from the lungs is blocked, pressure builds and suddenly released, producing a plosive sound usually associated with the letters p, t, k, b, d, and g, and in English words like pat, kid, and bag.

Plover A small-billed, gregarious wading bird typically found in water.

Plucked To rob or fleece.

Plumeria A fragrant, flowering tropical tree.

Plummet A plumb or a plumb line.

Plumped Bulging, as with contents, full.

Plumping To express support for something or someone.

Plumps To shake or pat to make rounded and soft, e.g., to plump the stuffing of a cushion.

Plus fours Baggy knickers reaching below the knee worn by men, especially when playing golf.

Plush A rich fabric of silk, cotton, or wool, or combination of these with a long, soft nap.

Plussed Calm, collected and unconfused; cf. nonplussed.

Plute An informal term for a plutocrat; a moveable shield used alongside siege engines in ancient Roman warfare.

Pneuma Greek, for neuter.

Pneumatics Those who are spiritual.

Pneumatique A letter or message transmitted by pneumatic dispatch.

Poesis The activity in which a person brings something into being that did not exist before.

Poetaster A person who writes inferior poetry.

Poète maudit A poet who is insufficiently appreciated by their contemporaries.

Poilus An infantry soldier in the French army, especially one who fought in World War One.

Point d'appui A location where troops are assembles prior to a battle.

Pointillism A technique of painting in which small, distinct dots of color are applied in patterns to form an image; cf. pointillistic.

Pointillistic Composed of many discrete details or parts; relating to pointillism; cf. pointillism.

Poire A flathead.

Poky Annoyingly slow or dull; a room uncomfortably small and cramped.

Poleaxe A battle ax with a short handle and often a hook or spike opposite a blade; cf. poleaxed.

Poleaxed To kill or knock down with a poleaxe; to cause great shock to someone; cf. poleaxe.

Poll   A person or animal's head.

Pollexfen   A highly attractive vibrant person full of life who is uplifting, inspiring and charming.

Polonia   people of Polish descent living outside Poland.

Polonius   A garrulous courtier and father of Ophelia and Laertes in Shakespeare's *Hamlet*.

Poltroon   A spiritless coward, craven; cf. craven.

Polyanthus   An herbaceous flowering plant which is a hybrid between wild primrose and primulas cultivated in Europe since the 17th century.

Polygonal   A plane figure with at least three straight sides and angles, and typically five or more.

Polygynia   Polygamy, in which a man has more than one wife.

Polygyny   The most common and accepted form of polygamy with the marriage of a man with several women.

Polyhister   Same as polymath; a person of wide-ranging knowledge or learning

Polyphony   The style of simultaneously combining a number of parts, each forming an individual melody and harmonizing with the other.

Polysemism   Capable of having several possible meanings.

Polysemous   Having multiple meanings.

Pomade A scented ointment applied to the hair or scalp.

Pomatum A scented ointment or oil applied to the hair, pomade.

Pommel A rounded knob on the end of the handle of a sword, dagger, or gun; the upward curving part of a saddle in front of the rider.

Pompadour A woman's hairstyle where the hair is turned back off the forehead in a roll.

Pompe funèbre A funeral ceremony or rites.

Pone Baked or fried bread made of corn and another ingredient like sweet potato, common in the thirteen colonies and the southern United States.

Poop The aftermost and highest deck of a ship, especially in a sailing ship where it typically forms the roof of the cabin in the stern.

Popish A derogatory term for a Roman Catholic.

Popoule "Madame Popoule" is a painting by Henri de Toulouse Lautrec depicting an aging woman pondering her faded beauty.

Poppycorn Annual, red-flowered Eurasian poppy common in fields and cultivated in several varieties, also known as corn poppy.

Poppysmik The sound from smacking the lips.

Porcine Resembling a pig; pig-like.

Porkpie hat   A hat with a low telescoped crown, flat top, and flexible brim.

Porksteak   Steak cut from the shoulder of a pig.

Poros   A coarse limestone found in the Peloponnesus and used extensively as building material by the ancient Greeks.

Porphyritic   In geology, relating to a rock texture, typically found in volcanic rocks, containing crystalline particles.

Porphyry   A hard, igneous rock containing crystals, usually feldspar, finely ground, typically reddish groundmass.

Port cochere   A covered entrance large enough for vehicles to pass through, typically opening into a courtyard.

Portia   The rich, beautiful, and intelligent heiress in Shakespeare's *Merchant of Venice*.

Portmanteau   A large trunk or suitcase, typically made of leather; a word blending the sounds and combining the meanings of two other words, e. g., *motel* from *motor* and *hotel*.

Posse comitatus   Frequently shortened to posse, a group of people mobilized by a sheriff to suppress lawlessness or defend the country.

Posset   A cold dessert made from thickened cream, typically flavored with lemon; regurgitated curdled milk (of a baby).

Post hoc ergo propter hoc   The fallacy of thinking that one event causes another event, also known as the post hoc fallacy.

Postilion A person who rides the leading left-hand horse of a team or pair driving a coach or carriage.

Postprandial The period after lunch or dinner; occurring after a meal.

Postum A powdered, roasted grain beverage popular as a coffee substitute.

Posy A poser, especially in being trendy or fashionable in a superficial way.

Potation A drink; the action of drinking alcohol; a drinking bout.

Potemkin Village From Russian Prince Potemkin describing an undesirable reality hidden behind an impressive façade designed to deceive observers into thinking their reality is better than it actually is.

Pother A commotion or fuss.

Poulet A love letter.

Poultice A soft, moist mass of material, typically of a plant or flour, applied to the body to relieve soreness and inflammation.

Pourparler Discussion prior to negotiations.

Praecox Latin for *very early* such as "praecox flowering."

Praemunire The offense of asserting or maintaining papal jurisdiction in England.

Pram A four-wheeled baby carriage.

Praxis Practice, as distinguished from theory.

Prelapsarian Characteristic of the time before the Fall of Man; innocent and unspoiled.

Prelate A bishop or other high ecclesiastical dignitary.

Pre-natal Before giving birth; cf. perinatal.

Prepense Deliberate, intentional.

Prephylloxera Rare vines that were devastated in Europe by phylloxera; cf. phylloxera.

Prepossess To impress favorably.

Prequel A story or movie containing events that precede those of an existing work.

Presidio *In Spain,* a fortified military settlement.

Prestonpans A small town in southeast Scotland on the Firth of Forth where the Jacobite army of Prince Charles Edward defeated government forces in 1745.

Preterite Expressing a past action or state.

Pretermit Legally to omit to do or mention; to abandon for a time (like a custom).

Preternatural Beyond what is normal or natural.

Prevenance   Attentiveness to or anticipation of others' needs or an instance of such anticipation, consideration.

Prevision   A feeling or prediction about a future event.

Prig   A self-righteously moralistic person who behaves as if superior to others.

Prim decorum   Precise or proper to the point of affection, excessively decorous, straight-laced, prudish; neat, and trim.

Primus interpares   *Latin for* first among equals; the senior or representative member of a group.

Priscian   To break Priscian's head means to violate the rules of grammar. Priscian was a great 5th-century grammarian whose name is synonymous with grammar.

Prise   To use force to move, part, or open something; to obtain something from someone with effort or difficulty.

Prisiadka   A dance step executed by extending the legs alternately forward from a squatting position; cf. trepak.

Prius   Something that precedes or takes precedence; a precondition.

Privily   *Archaic for* in a secret way.

Prix fixe   A meal consisting of several courses served at a fixed price.

Prix Volney   The Volney Prize is awarded by the Institute of France for a work of comparative philology.

Pro patria mori To die.

Pro tempore Often shortened to pro temp, for the time being; lasting only for the time being.

Proclus A Greek Neoplatonist philosopher and one of the last major classical philosophers of antiquity.

Prodesse *In Latin*, where the verb is at the end of the sentence so the reader is held in suspense until the last word.

Proem The opening or introduction to a speech.

Profane Relating or devoted to that which is not sacred or biblical, secular rather than religious; disrespectful of orthodox religious practice, irreverent.

Prognathous Having a projecting lower jaw or chin; projecting; having projecting mouthparts.

Prolegomenon A critical or discursive introduction to a book.

Prolix *In speech or writing*, using too many words, tediously lengthy.

Prolonge *In the military*, a rope having a hook at one end and a toggle at the other used for various purposes such as to draw a gun carriage.

Prone Lying face down; cf. supine.

Propaedeutic An area of study serving as a preliminary instruction or as an introduction to further study; an introduction to a subject or area of study.

Propinquity The state of being close to someone or something; proximity; close kinship; cf. apropinquity.

Propontis The small inland sea that connects the Aegean Sea to the Black Sea, historically called the Sea of Marmara.

Propylaea The structure forming the entrance to a temple.

Prorogation The action of discontinuing a session of a legislative assembly without dissolving it.

Prorogue To discontinue of session of a legislative assembly without dissolving it.

Prosaism A prosaic manner, style or quality; a prosaic expression.

Proserpine in Hades *In classical mythology,* the goddess of springtime and queen of the underworld.

Prosit *German for* may it be beneficial or be well, used when toasting to a person's health.

Proslogium *Latin for* discourse on the existence of God; a discourse.

Prosodic Relating to the rhythm and intonation, or the way a speaker's voice rises and falls, of language.

Prosody The patterns of rhythm and sound used in poetry.

Prosopographic A description of a person's social and family connections and career.

Prosopopoeial A figure of speech in which an abstract thing is personified; a figure of speech in which an imagined or absent person or thing is represented as speaking.

Prospect A broad view; a scene.

Prostyle A portico with a maximum of four columns.

Prosy Showing no imagination; commonplace or dull.

Protectograph A check writer; a machine that prints on a check to authenticate that the check is genuine.

Prothalamion A song or poem celebrating an upcoming wedding.

Prothonotary A chief clerk in some courts of law.

Proto Original or primitive.

Prototypical The first, original, or typical form of something.

Prunella A plant cultivated for medicine, ground cover and rock garden plants; *in clothing*, a worsted fabric made with a blend of silk.

Prurient Having excessive interest in sexual matters.

Prussic An acid called so because Prussian blue is derived from it or its compounds, now called hydrocyanic acid.

Psalmist The author or composer of psalms, especially of biblical psalms.

Psalter A copy of the biblical Psalms, especially for liturgical use; cf. liturgical.

Psaltery A medieval musical instrument like a dulcimer but played by plucking the strings with the fingers or a plectrum.

Psammophile A plant or animal that prefers or thrives in sandy areas.

Psephologist One who studies psephology; cf. psephology.

Psephology A branch of political science that statistically studies elections and trends in voting.

Pseudoperipteral A classical Greek building with engaged columns embedded in the outer walls except the front of the building.

Psychostasis *In religion*, the weighing of souls before and after death to judge a person's fate.

Ptomaine poisoning Obsolete term for food poisoning caused by ingesting ptomaine, cf. ptomaine.

Ptomaine Putrefying animal or vegetable matter formerly thought to cause food poisoning, contaminated food, cf. ptomaine poisoning.

Ptosis The drooping or falling of the upper eyelid.

Publican *In ancient Roman and biblical times*, a tax collector.

Puce A dark red or purple-brown color.

Puerta A city gate.

Puissance A competitive test of a horse's ability to jump large obstacles; archaic for great power, influence or prowess.

Puissant Archaic for having great power or influence.

Puling To cry like a chicken; whining or whimpering.

Pulling *British for* to hook up with someone or make out with them, often at a party or nightclub.

Pulmonary consumption An old, once common term for the wasting away of the body, particularly from pulmonary tuberculosis, other old terms include the King's evil, scrofula, and Pott's disease.

Pulmotor A rigid case fitted over a patient's body, used for artificial respiration by means of mechanical pumps; an iron lung.

Pulpy Resembling or consisting of pulp, mushy; in writing sensationalist or poor quality, trashy.

Pung A low box sleigh drawn by a horse.

Pungy A two-masted schooner for oyster dredging or fishing in Chesapeake Bay, also called a Chesapeake canoe.

Punkah A large cloth fan on a frame suspended from the ceiling, moved by pulling a cord; common in India.

Purblind Having impaired or defective vision; to be slow or unable to understand, dimwitted.

Purebred   Bred from parents of the same breed or variety; cf. thoroughbred.

Purle   Obsolete spelling of pearl; ale or beer spiced with wormwood or other bitter herbs, regarded as a tonic; one who spellchecks and corrects grammar.

Purlieu   The area near or surrounding a place; historically, a tract on the border of a forest, especially one earlier included in and still partly subject to forest laws.

Purling   The motion of a small stream among obstructions; flowing with a murmuring sound.

Purple prose (or writing)   Prose that is so extravagant, ornate, or flowery it breaks the flow and draws excessive attention to itself; overly melodramatic and fanciful.

Purse-proud   Proud of one's wealth, especially in an arrogant or showy manner.

Puseyism   The theological doctrine of the English theologian Edward Posey in the Oxford Movement; cf. Tractarianism.

Puseyite   A follower of Puseyism; cf. Puseyism.

Putlanesca   A pasta sauce typically including tomatoes, garlic, olives and anchovies.

Puttee   A long strip of cloth wound spirally around the leg from the ankle to knee for protection and support; a leather legging.

Putti (or putto)   A representation of a naked child, especially a cherub or cupid in Renaissance art.

Pyorrhea Another term for periodontitis, or inflammation of the tissue around the teeth often causing shrinkage of the guns and loosening of the teeth.

Python A high-level, general-purpose programming language.

Q

Quackish   Characteristic of a quack; boastfully pretentious.

Quadriga   A chariot drawn by four horses abreast, favored in classical antiquity and the Roman Empire.

Quadrivium   *In ancient education*, consisting of arithmetic, geometry, music, and astronomy; cf. trivium.

Quadroon   A person who is one-quarter black.

Quail   To lose heart or courage in difficulty or danger; to shrink with fear; to recoil, flinch, blench, or cower.

Quartan ague   From Anglo-Norman and Old French, a mild form of malaria causing a fever that recurs every third day.

Quarter-face   A face turned away (such as in a portrait) so only one quarter is visible.

Quarto   The size of a book page resulting from folding each printed sheet into four leaves (eight pages).

Quatrain   A stanza of four lines, especially one having alternate rhymes.

Quatrefoil   An ornamental design of four lobes or leaves used in architectural tracery resembling a flower or four-leaf clover.

Quell   To put an end to, like a rebellion, typically by force; to subdue or silence someone; to suppress, especially unpleasant feelings.

Querent   An inquirer; one who consults an astrologer.

Querist   *Archaic*, a person who asks questions; a questioner.

Querulous   Excessively talkative, especially on trivial matters; habitually complaining, peevish.

Quid   One pound sterling.

Quien sabe   *Spanish for* who knows.

Quiesce   To become quiet, calm or silent.

Quire   *In medieval manuscripts*, four sheets of paper or parchment folded to form eight leaves; any collection of leaves, one within another, in a manuscript or book.

Quirinal   Designating or relating the northernmost of the traditional seven hills of Rome, or a building or institution on this hill.

Quoin   An external angle of a wall or building.

R

Rachitic   Pertaining to or affected by rickets; feeble; in a weak precarious condition.

Rack   To cause physical or mental pain or trouble to someone or something.

Raffole   To adore, to be mad about.

Raison d'être   The most important reason or purpose for someone or something's existence.

Ramifying   To form branches or offshoots.

Ranke   A tendril or shoot.

Rann   A stanza, especially of a song.

Rape   Also called rapeseed or colza; a plant of the mustard family whose seeds yield canola oil and ingredients for soap.

Rappee   A strong snuff made from dark, coarse tobacco.

Rapporteur   A person appointed by an organization to report on the proceedings of its meetings.

Ratafia A liqueur flavored with almonds or kernels of peaches, apricots, or cherries.

Rath Pre-historic hill forts associated with folklore and fairies.

Ratio studiorum A document that standardized the globally influential system of Jesuit education in 1599.

Ratline A series of small ropes fastened across a sailing ship's shrouds like the rungs of a ladder, used for climbing rigging.

Ratskeller A bar or restaurant located in the basement of a city hall or nearby.

Raven Black hair with blue undertones.

Ravening Extremely hungry and hunting for prey.

Real trick Being or occurring in fact or actuality; having a verified existence; a cunning or deceitful action or device.

Reanimate To restore to life or consciousness; to revive.

Rebuse A puzzle in which words are represented by combinations of pictures and individual letters, apex, for example, might be represented by a picture of an ape followed by the letter x, also spelled rebus.

Recherché Rare, exotic, or obscure.

Recitative *In music*, a dialogue sung in rhythm with ordinary speech with many words on the same note.

Réclame   Public acclaim; notoriety.

Recrudescence   The recurrence of an undesirable condition.

Rectilinear   Relating to a straight line or lines.

Recto   The right or front side of an open book; cf. verso.

Recursion   A phrase that contains an example of itself.

Recursive   Characterized by recurrence or repetition.

Recur   To have recourse to; an event that happens repeatedly.

Recurve   *In Biology*, to bend backwards; in archery, a bow that curves forward at the ends, which straighten out under tension when the bow is drawn.

Recusancy   A person who refuses to submit to an authority or to comply with a regulation.

Recusant   A person who refuses to submit to an authority or to comply with regulations.

Red tapist   One who strictly adheres to official formalities.

Redan   A V-shaped embankment extending from and forming a part of a fortification.

Redound   To contribute greatly to a person's credit or honor.

Reeperbahn   The center of a city's nightlife that often includes a red-light district.

Refractory Stubborn or unmanageable; resistant to a process, stimulus, or change.

Refrain A line or lines that are repeated in music or in poetry.

Refrange To break or tear.

Regisseur A director responsible for staging a theatrical work.

Regius *Latin*, A king; of or belonging to a king; holding a chair in a university founded or dependent on a sovereign.

Reify To make something more concrete or real.

Relict A thing that has survived from an earlier period; *archaic for* a widow.

Render To cause to be or become, to make.

Rentier A person living on income from property or investments.

Rent To separate in parts with force or violence; to tear.

Repayther A type of clock mechanism called a repeater.

Repechage A sports contest where the best-placed of those who failed to win compete for second place in the final.

Repoussé *In metalwork*, hammered into relief from the reverse side.

Reprove To reprimand or censure.

Res et verba *In Latin*, things, facts or actions instead of words.

Rescript An official edict or announcement (historically a Roman Emperor's legal reply or the Pope's decision on a question of papal law).

Retailed To relate or repeat something, especially a story, in detail.

Retail To pass information to other people, especially personal details about someone.

Retch To make the sound and movement of vomiting; a movement or sound of vomiting.

Reticule A woman's small handbag, originally netted and typically having a drawstring and decorated with embroidery or beading.

Retiracy Retirement, seclusion.

Retrograde Directed or moving backward; to go back in position or time; a degenerate person.

Revanche A policy or movement aimed at achieving the return of a nation's lost territory.

Reverie A state of being pleasantly lost in one's thoughts, a daydream; *in music,* an instrumental piece suggesting a dreamy or musing state; *archaic for* a fanciful or impractical idea or theory.

Revetment A retaining wall or facing of masonry supporting or protecting a rampart or wall.

Rex   The reigning king, used following a name or in the titles of lawsuits like Rex. V. Smith or the Crown versus Smith.

Rhadamanthus   A wise king of Crete said to be one of the judges of the dead.

Rheumatism   Any disease marked by inflammation and pain in the joints, muscles, or fibrous tissue, especially in rheumatoid arthritis.

Rhombus   Any parallelogram with equal sides, including a square.

Rill   A small stream.

Rime   A frost formed on cold objects by rapid freezing of water vapor in a cloud or fog; to cover an object with hoarfrost; cf. hoarfrost.

Ritualism   *In Christianity*, emphasizing the rituals and liturgical ceremonies of the church; the regular observance or practice of ritual, especially when excessive or without regard to its function.

Riven   To split or tear violently.

Road to Damascus   A turning point, a life-changing experience; refers to the biblical story of Saul who converted to Christianity on his way to Damascus.

Roan   An animal, especially a horse or cow, having a coat of a main color thickly interspersed with hairs of another color.

Rococo Exceptionally ornamental and theatrical style of art that combines asymmetry, scrolling curves, gilding, and white and pastel colors.

Rodomontade Boastful or inflated talk or behavior.

Roe A small Eurasian deer that lacks a tail and has a reddish summer coat that turns grayish in the winter.

Roister To enjoy oneself or celebrate boisterously.

Roman à clef A novel in which real people or events appear with invented names.

Romans à these A didactic novel or one that expounds a theory.

Roorback A defamatory falsehood published for political effect.

Roseate Rose-colored; optimistic or idealistic.

Rota A list showing when each of a number of people are to do a particular job; the supreme ecclesiastical and secular court in the Roman Catholic Church.

Rotogravure A printing system using a rotary press with intaglio cylinders running at high speed, used for long print runs of magazines and stamps.

Roué A debauched man, especially an elderly one.

Round hand Careful handwriting in which the letters are rounded, distinct, and full.

Roundsman   A police officer in charge of a patrol.

Rout   A kind of rich sweet cake made for routs, or evening parties.

Roux   A mixture of flour and fat cooked together and used to thicken sauces.

Rowel   A spiked, revolving disk at the end of a spur, usually used to urge on a horse.

Royster   To engage in noisy merrymaking, to revel; to brag, bluster, or swagger.

Rubberneck   To turn one's head to stare at something foolishly.

Ruben   A biblical Hebrew male first name meaning *behold, a son*; a country bumpkin; a tiller of the soil.

Rubicund   Having a ruddy, high-colored complexion, especially of someone's face.

Rubied   Having a color like deep ruby red.

Ruble   A rear, outside seat.

Ruche   A frill or pleat of fabric as decoration on a garment or home furnishing.

Rune   A letter of an ancient Germanic alphabet; cf. runic.

Runic   Consisting of runes in ancient northern European peoples; a secret or mysterious meaning; cf. rune.

Runnel   A narrow channel in the ground for liquid to flow through; a brook or rill; a small stream of a particular liquid.

Rusk   A light, dry biscuit or piece of twice-baked bread; cf. zwieback .

Russet   A reddish-brown color; *archaic for* rustic, homely.

Rusticated   To be sent down by a university for punishment for an academic or disciplinary lapse.

Rustication   To reside in the country or follow a rustic life; *British*, to be suspended from school or college; to build a face with unusually rough-surfaced masonry.

Rustic   Relating to the countryside, rural; made plainly and simply.

S

Sabe To know, to understand, or comprehend.

Sacaea An ancient five-day Babylonian festival identified with the Greek goddess Athena characterized by drunkenness and licentious behavior.

Sachem A boss or leader.

Sackbut An early form of trombone used in Renaissance music.

Sackcloth A rough, coarse fabric woven from flax or hemp; a religious token of mourning.

Sagamore In some North American Indian peoples, a chief.

Sake Out of consideration for or to help someone.

Sal volatile A scented solution of ammonium carbonate in alcohol used as smelling salts.

Salience Particularly noticeable or important; prominent.

Salient Of an angle pointing outward, like a piece of land or section of a fortification that juts out to form an angle.

Saline Salty, containing salt; swearing like a sailor or the use of language not fit for polite company.

Sallow An unhealthy yellow or pale brown color, as of a person's face or complexion.

Saltimbanco A quack doctor, a fraud.

Salva reverential A sincere and true apology.

Salver A tray, usually made of silver used for formal occasions.

Samizdat The clandestine copying and distribution of literature banned by the state, especially in formerly communist eastern European countries.

Samothrace A Greek island in the northern Aegean Sea.

Sanative Conducive to physical or spiritual health and well-being; healing.

Sandyx Red dye from oxides of lead and iron; scarlet cloth.

Sanger fest A singing festival.

Sang froid Composure or coolness under trying circumstances.

Sanguine Optimistic, confident.

Sanguis Latin for blood or bloodshed.

Sanitas sanitatum omnia sanitas From Benjamin Disraeli meaning the continuous order is the only parent of personal liberty and political right.

Santon An ascetic priest.

Sapolio A brand of soap noted for its advertising.

Sap Palm sap begins fermenting wine immediately, making it mildly intoxicating and sweet.

Saprolegnia An aquatic fungus that attacks fish and other aquatic animals.

Sap roller *In the military*, a large gabion, six or seven feet long, filled with fascines, which the sapper rolls along before him for protection from enemy fire.

Saracenic A member of a pre-Islamic nomadic people of the Syrian and Arabian Deserts; a Muslim, especially of the time of the Crusades.

Sarcastrophe A triangle symbol around words or sentences to denote sarcasm, e.g. *It never rains in England..*

Sard A yellow or brownish-red variety of chalcedony; cf. sardonyx, onyx, chalcedony.

Sardonic Disdainfully or skeptically humorous; derisively mocking.

Sardonyx An onyx in which layers alternate with sard; cf. onyx, sard.

Saurian   Like a lizard; any large reptile, especially a dinosaur or other extinct form.

Sauterne   A sweet white wine from Sauternes in the Bordeaux region of France.

Savile Row   A street in Mayfair, central London, known principally for its tailoring of men.

Scabland   *In geology*, flat, elevated, and deeply scarred by glacial channel areas with poor soil and little vegetation.

Scabrous   Rough and covered with scabs; indecent, salacious.

Scallion   A long-necked onion with a small bulb, in particular a green onion.

Scapegrace   A mischievous or wayward person, especially a young person or child; a rascal.

Scapular   Relating to the shoulder or shoulder blade; a short monastic cloak covering the shoulders.

Scarab   A large dung beetle of the eastern Mediterranean area regarded as sacred in ancient Egypt.

Schadenfreude   Pleasure derived by someone from another person's misfortune.

Schemata   A representation or a plan or theory in the form of an outline or model; a syllogistic figure.

Schlemiel   A Yiddish term for an inept, incompetent person; a fool.

Scholiast A commentator on ancient or classical literature.

Schoolman A teacher.

Schottische A slow polka dance.

Scientism Thoughts or expressions regarded as characteristic of scientists.

Scimitar A short sword with a curved blade that broadens toward the point, used mostly in Eastern countries.

Sciolist A person who pretends to be knowledgeable and well-informed.

Scofflaw A person who flouts the law, especially by failing to comply with laws that are difficult to enforce.

Scoff To speak to someone scornfully, derisively, or mockingly.

Sconce A candle holder that is attached to a wall with an ornamental bracket.

Scoon To skim or skip across water like a flat stone.

Scoria A cindery, vesicular basaltic lava typically having a frothy texture.

Scortia *In classical architecture,* concave molding, especially at the base of a column.

Scow A smaller type of barge, sometimes rigged for sailing, used on inland waterways due to their ability to navigate shallow water.

Scrannel To be slight, lean, or thin.

Scrim A strong, coarse fabric used for heavy-duty lining or upholstery; *in theater*, gauze that appears opaque until lit from behind; a heatproof cloth put over film to diffuse light.

Scrimshaw Scrollwork, engravings or carvings done in bone or ivory.

Scrofula A disease, probably from tuberculosis with glandular swellings.

Scruple A feeling of doubt or hesitation due to morality or propriety; to hesitate or be reluctant to do something one thinks may be wrong.

Scud A formation of vapory clouds driven fast by the wind.

Scull A pair of small oars used by a single rower.

Scullion A servant assigned the most menial kitchen tasks.

Scuppernong A variety of the muscadine grape native to the Scuppernong River in North Carolina; a wine made from the scuppernong grape.

Scurrilous Making or spreading scandalous claims about someone with the intention of damaging their reputation.

Scurvy A disease caused by a deficiency of vitamin C characterized by swollen, bleeding gums and the opening of previously healed wounds that particularly affected poorly nourished sailors in the 18th century; worthless or contemptible.

Scutcheon   A shield, especially one displaying a coat of arms.

Scylla   *In mythology*, a female monster with six snake-like heads, each with pointed teeth.

Scytale   A Spartan short club or cudgel.

Sebastopol   The largest city in Crimea and major port on the Black Sea that has been an important naval port throughout history due to its strategic location.

Secesh   A secessionist; a supporter of the Confederacy during the United States Civil War.

Secret du roi   Secret diplomacy; for twenty years, King Louis XV split his diplomacy into official and secret channels.

Secretary   *In Latin*, "confidential officer;" a confidant, entrusted with private or secret matters.

Sectarian   Concerning a sect or sects; a member of a sect; cf. sectarianism.

Sectarianism   Political or cultural conflict between two groups, often political.

Sectaries   A member of a religious or political sect.

Sedan   An enclosed chair for conveying a person, carried between horizontal poles by two or more porters.

Sedulous   Showing dedication and diligence, to apply oneself.

See   A bet or challenge.

Seiche   A standing wave in an enclosed or partially enclosed body of water.

Seine   A fishing net that hangs vertically in the water with floats at the top and weights at the bottom, drawn together to encircle the fish.

Sejanus   An ambitious ancient Roman soldier (20 B.C. to A.D. 31) and friend of Roman Emperor Tiberius.

Selah   A word that occurs in the Hebrew Bible many times whose meaning is uncertain, but is probably a musical mark or an instruction to stop and listen.

Semele   *In Greek mythology*, the daughter of Cadmus who was consumed by flames when she visited Zeus.

Semiotician   An expert in or student of semiotics; cf. semiotics.

Semiotic   Relating to signs and symbols.

Semiotics   The study of signs and symbols and their use or interpretation.

Sempiternal   Eternal and unchanging; everlasting.

Sempronian   *Latin for* always, continuously, at any time, for a long time.

Senectus   *Latin for* old age.

Senescence The condition or process of deterioration with age.

Sennacherib King of Assyria (705-681) who invaded Judah twice and defeated Babylon.

Sephardic A Jew who is descended from the Jews who lived on the Iberian Peninsula.

Seps A legendary snake from medieval bestiaries said to have extremely corrosive venom that liquefied their prey; an African lizard with a body resembling a snake.

Sept An Irish clan; a clan.

Septuagenarian A person who is from 70 to 79 years old.

Sepulchral Relating to a tomb or internment; gloomy, dismal.

Sequacious Following in a regular sequence; ready to follow any leader, pliant; lacking independence or originality of thought.

Sequitur The conclusion of an inference, the consequence.

Seraph An angelic being who in Christian angelology belongs to the highest order of the nine-fold celestial hierarchy associated with light, ardor and purity.

Sere Dry or withered.

Serge A durable, twilled woolen or worsted fabric.

Seria A large earthenware jar.

Seriatim   Taking one subject after another in regular order, point by point.

Sericulture   Silk farming, the cultivation of silkworms to produce silk.

Serio   Serious.

Sermo vulgus   Common speech.

Serrate   Notched or toothed on the edge; cf. crenulated.

Serried   Rows of people or things standing close together.

Servitor   A person who serves or attends a social superior; an Oxford University undergraduate. performing menial duties in exchange for assistance from the college.

Setebo   A supposed deity of the Patagonians alluded to in Shakespeare's *The Tempest.*

Setpiece   A self-contained passage or section of a novel, play, or music arranged in an elaborate or conventional pattern for maximum effect; British for a carefully organized and practiced move in a team game by which the ball is returned to play.

Seven Sleepers   *In Christian and Islamic mythology,* a group of youths who hid inside a cave outside of the city of Ephesus around A.D. 250 to escape religious persecution and emerged 300 years later.

Sexton   A person who looks after a church, sometimes acting as a bell-ringer or gravedigger.

Sfumato   The painting technique of allowing tones and colors to blend gradually into one another, producing softened outlines or hazy forms.

Shades   *In mythology*, a spirit or ghost of a dead person residing in the underworld.

Shako   A cylindrical military hat with a brim and plume.

Shandygaff   Beer diluted with a nonalcoholic drink such as ginger beer.

Shank   A person's leg, especially the part from the knee to the ankles.

Sheave   A sheaf, a bundle of grain stalks laid lengthwise and tied together for reaping.

Sheering   To swerve or change course quickly, typically with a boat; to avoid something unpleasant such as a person, thing, or topic.

Shem and Shaun   Brothers in the novel *Finnegan's Wake* who are utter opposites.

Shemozzle   A state of chaos and confusion; a muddle.

Sherbet   A cooling drink of sweet, diluted fruit juices.

Sherd   Another word for potsherd; a broken piece of ceramic material, especially one found at an archaeological site.

Shibboleth   A custom, principle, or belief distinguishing a particular class or group of people, especially a longstanding one, regarded as outmoded or no longer important.

Shift A woman's loose, shirt-like undergarment; a loose-fitting dress that hangs straight.

Shillelagh A thick stick of blackthorn or oak used in Ireland for walking or as a weapon.

Shilling To talk about or describe someone or something in a favorable way because you are being paid to do it.

Shindy A noisy disturbance or quarrel.

Shingle A mass of small, rounded pebbles, especially on seashore; a painful viral infection that causes a painful rash that looks like a shingle.

Shinola An obsolete brand of boot polish; a euphemism for "shit."

Shiver A splinter of something broken, like a small piece of broken glass; to shatter.

Shoat A young pig, especially one newly weaned.

Shotted Filled or weighted with shot.

Shying To throw something suddenly, often sideways.

Shy To suddenly show fright at an object, noise, or movement, especially a horse; a sudden, startled movement.

Sibilant Having or producing the sound resembling an 's' or 'sh' as in sash.

Sibyl *In ancient times,* a woman who is supposed to foretell the oracles and prophecies of God.

Sickle   Shaped like a sickle; crescent-shaped.

Sieur   A formal or polite term for a man; archaically, a gentleman of high social status.

Sigmoid   Curved like a "C;" crescent-shaped; S-shaped.

Silage   Grass or green fodder compacted and stored in airtight conditions used as animal feed; preserved grass.

Silene   A large and widely distributed genus of plants having showy flowers of various colors.

Silenus   *In Greek mythology,* a drunken martyr.

Silesia   A region in central Europe along both banks of the upper Oder River, mainly in southwest Poland and the north Czech Republic.

Silphium   An extinct Libyan wonder plant used for food and medicine.

Silviculture   The growing and cultivation of trees.

Silviculturist   One who practices silviculture; a forester.

Simba   A large, gregarious, predatory female mammal.

Simile   A figure of speech involving the comparison of one thing with another thing of a different kind for emphasis (e. g. a *brave lion*); cf. metaphor.

Simoom   A hot, dry, dust-laden wind blowing in the desert, especially in Arabia.

Simper   To smile in an affected, coy, or ingratiating manner.

Sine qua non   An essential condition; an absolutely necessary thing.

Sinecure   A position requiring little or no work but giving the holder a financial benefit.

Singlet   An under-shirt.

Siroccos   The hot and often dusty and rainy wind that blows from North Africa across the Mediterranean to southern Europe.

Skate   To pass over or refer fleetingly to a subject or problem; to glide, coast, flow, glissade; to shirk one's duty; to loaf.

Skein   A tangled or complicated arrangement, state or situation; a flock of wild geese or swans in flight, typically in a V-shaped formation.

Skeow   An exclamation, popularized by rednecks, for something utterly meaningless.

Skiey   Relating to the sky.

Skyphos   *In Greek*, a two-handled, deep wine cup on a low flanged base or none.

Slackjaw   Wearisome or imprudent talk.

Slang   Language that consists of informal words and phrases typically restricted to a particular group of people (cf. cant); to attack using abusive language.

Slanguage   Slangy speech or writing.

Slattern   A dirty, untidy woman.

Slavey   A member of a Dene people of northwestern Canada.

Sling   To throw or fling; a speaker's casual attitude.

Sloe-eyed   Having attractive, dark, typically almond-shaped eyes.

Sludgy   Muddy, soft wet earth, slimy.

Slumgullion   Cheap or insubstantial stew.

Sly-boot   Asly, a tricky person, especially one who is cunning or mischievous in an engaging way.

Smearcase   Any soft cheese suitable for spreading or eating with a spoon, especially sour cottage cheese.

Smilax   A widely distributed climbing shrub with hooks and tendrils; climbing asparagus used as a decorative by florists.

Snnacherib   King of Assyria who invaded Judea twice and defeated Babylon and rebuilt Nineveh after it had been destroyed by the Babylonians; died in 681 B.C.

Socinian   An adherent of the 16[th-] and 17th-century theological movement professing belief in God and adherence to the Christian Scriptures but denying the divinity of Christ.

Sockdolager   A forceful blow; an exceptional person or thing.

Sodalicious   Delicious in a way that involves or resembles soda.

Soever   Of any kind; to any extent.

Sol   A colloid made out of solid particles in a continuous liquid medium such as in blood, pigmented ink, and paint; cf. solation.

Sola topi   An Indian sun hat made from the pity of the stems of sola plants, a pith helmet; cf. topi.

Solas   Joy, pleasure happiness; The International Convention for the Safety of Life at Sea which is an international maritime treaty that sets standards for merchant ships.

Solation   The process of changing to a sol; cf. sol.

Solecism   A grammatical mistake in speech or writing; a breach of good manners, incorrect behavior.

Solent   A person or thing that shows the existence or direction of a trend; a strait of the English Channel between the coast of Hampshire and the Isle of Wight.

Solferino   A moderate, purplish-red color.

Soliloquy   The act of speaking one's thoughts aloud when alone, especially by a character in a play.

Sommelier   A wine steward; someone knowledgeable about fine dining.

Somnolence   The state of being drowsy; sleepiness.

Sonorous An imposingly deep and full sound, as in a person's voice.

Sop A thing of no great value, done as a concession to appease someone; a piece of bread dipped in gravy, soup, or sauce.

Sophia Wisdom.

Sophrosyne Temperance, self-control, moderation.

Sorbet A frozen dessert made from sweetened water with flavoring.

Sorrel A European plant of the dock family with arrow-shaped leaves that are used in salads and cooking for their acidic flavor.

Soteriological The doctrine of salvation.

Sotto voce Singing or speaking in a quiet voice, as if not to be overheard.

Soubrette An actress playing a lively, flirtatious role in a play.

Soupcon A very small quantity of something.

Span A pair of horses or other animals driven together.

Spandrel The triangular space between one side of the outer curve of an arch, wall, and the ceiling or framework.

Spanner A wrench.

Spate A large number; a sudden heavy rain.

Spatium The unlimited three-dimensional expanse in which all material objects are located.

Spavined Affected with swelling; old and decrepit.

Spencer *Chiefly British;* a steward or administrator.

Spenser, Edmund A 16th-century English poet best known for *The Faerie Queene*, an epic poem celebrating the Tudor dynasty and Elizabeth I.

Spick Pejorative word for a Latin American.

Spilt milk To feel sorry or sad about something that has already happened, used to emphasize that this is not helpful.

Spirituelle Witty.

Spittle Saliva, especially that ejected from the mouth.

Splat A thin piece of wood in the center of a chair back.

Splenetic Bad-tempered, spiteful.

Splinter net In nautical terms, netting formed of small rope rigged on a man-of-war to prevent accidents from splinters and falling spars in action.

Split infinitive A construction consisting of an infinitive with an adverb or other word inserted between *to* and the verb, e.g. she seems to really like it.

Spoink A fishy, vaginal odor.

Spondaic *In prosody*, a foot consisting of two long (stressed) syllables.

Spondulix 19th-century slang for money or cash, specifically a reasonable amount of spending money.

Spooney A softy; to soften.

Spoon Someone silly, foolish; to be shallow, uninformed, or dumb.

Spoor The track or scent of an animal; to follow the track or scent of an animal or person.

Spraddle To spread the legs far apart.

Spray Large, flat bouquets of long-stemmed plant material; to urinate on various objects as a way of marketing territory.

Spritz To squirt or spray something at or onto something in quick, short bursts; the act of squirting or spraying in quick short bursts.

Squint To have eyes that look in different directions; a quick or casual look; cf. strabismus.

Squirearchy Landowners collectively, especially when considered as a class having political or social influence.

Squireen A petty squire; a gentleman in a small way.

Stacking Serving alcoholic drinks before a customer is done with their current one.

Stake side An extra-large cargo area.

Stale   To urinate.

Stanhope   A light, one-horse, four-wheeled carriage.

Stanza   A group of lines forming the basic recurring metrical unit in a poem or verse; in some Greek and Latin meters, a group of four lines.

Starosty   *In Poland,* a castle and domain conferred on a nobleman for life.

Stasimon   *In Greek tragedy,* a stationary song composed of strophes and antistrophes and performed by the chorus or orchestra.

Stasis theory   A pre-writing, four-question process developed by Aristotle and Hermagoras where writers are asked for the facts, the nature of the issue, the seriousness of the issue and any objections.

Stasis   Civil strife; a state that does not change.

Status quo ante bellum   *Latin for* the situation as it existed before the war; cf. status quo ante.

Stave   A narrow length of wood with a slightly beveled edge to form the sides of barrels, tanks, tubs, vats, and pipelines.

Stein   A large mug used especially for beer; the quantity of beer that a stein holds.

Stele   The central core of the stem and root of a vascular plant consisting of vascular tissue and supporting tissue.

Stem winder   An entertaining and rousing speech; a watch wound by turning a knob on the end of a stem.

Stereopticon   A slide projector that combines two images to create a three-dimensional effect.

Stertorous   Noisy and labored breathing.

Stipple   *In drawing, painting and engraving*, to mark with numerous small dots or specks.

Stipt   Punctual, arriving on time, not late.

Stoat   A small, carnivorous mammal of the weasel family with chestnut fur, white underparts and black-tipped tail native to Eurasia and North America; cf. ermine.

Stomacher   A V-shaped piece of decorative cloth, worn over the chest and belly by men and women in the 16th century, later only by women.

Stone   Fourteen pounds.

Storm and stress   A phrase coined by psychologist G. Stanley Hall, to refer to the period of adolescence as a time of turmoil and difficulty that involves conflict with parents and authority, mood swings, and risky behavior.

Strabismus   The abnormal alignment of the eyes; the condition of having a squint; cf. squint.

Straightner   A doctor in Butler's book *Erewhon.*

Strand   The shore of a sea, lake, or large river.

Stratum A layer or a series of layers of rock in the ground; a thin layer within any structure.

Stresa The state of stress.

Stringcourse A raised, horizontal band or course of bricks on a building; cf. cordon.

Strum and Drang A literary and artistic movement in Germany in the late 18th century, influenced by Jean Jacques Rousseau and characterized by emotional unrest and rejection of neoclassical literary norms; turbulent emotion or stress.

Strumpet An early printed book, especially one printed before 1501 (when most books were written by hand).

Stube An establishment serving chiefly alcoholic beverages, especially beer.

Sty A pigpen.

Stygian shadow Relating to the River Styx, extremely dark, gloomy, or foreboding.

Style champêtre A genre of painting popular in France in the early-18th century characterized by pastoral settings.

Stylus A hard point, typically diamond, following a groove in a record and transmitting the recorded sound; an ancient writing implement consisting of a small rod with a pointed end for scratching letters on wax-covered tablets, and a blunt end for obliterating them.

Sub lunary Literally below the moon; denotes unchanging cosmos versus chaotic and fickle earth.

Sub Rosa Happening or done in secret.

Subaltern An officer in the British army below the rank of captain, especially a second lieutenant; of lower status; archaic in logic, a proposition that implies another proposition, with no implication in return.

Subjunctive A grammatical mood, a feature of the utterance that indicates the speaker's attitude toward it.

Sublunary Belonging to this world as opposed to a better or more spiritual one.

Subra Ancient Rome's Reeperbahn; cf. Reeperbahn.

Subvention A grant of money, especially from a government.

Succotash An American dish of corn and lima beans.

Succubi A female demon believed to have sexual intercourse with sleeping men; cf. incubus.

Sufficierit Enough, adequate.

Sufflate To blow up; to inflate; to inspire.

Suffusion To spread over or through in the manner of fluid or light; to flush, fill.

Sugaun Irish hay ropes.

Sui generis *Latin for* of its own kind, in a class by itself; unique.

Sulci A depression or furrow on the cerebral cortex; cf. gyrus.

Sumption The act of taking or assuming; a major premise of a syllogism.

Sunder To split apart.

Sunna The traditional portion of Muslim law based on Muhammad's words or acts as authoritative by the Muslims and followed particularly by Sunni Muslims; the orthodox Islamic community.

Supawn A boiled Indian meal; hasty pudding; mush.

Superadd To add something to what has already been added.

Superannuated Obsolete, old-fashioned, outmoded.

Supererogatory To do more than is asked for; the action of doing more than duty requires.

Superincumbent Lying or resting on someone else.

Superinduce To introduce as an addition over or above something already existing; to bring on, to induce.

Supernal Relating to the sky or heavens; celestial; of exceptional quality or extent.

Supernumerary Above the normal or requisite number.

Superscription Something written or engraved on the surface of something else; an inscription.

Supine Failing to act or protest as a result of moral weakness or indolence; lying face up; cf. prone.

Supplejack Any of various woody plant climbers having tough pliant stems, especially in the southern U.S.

Suppurate To generate pus.

Sur canapé To lie on a sofa or couch.

Surcease Cessation, to cease.

Surname A hereditary name common to all members of a family, as distinct from a given name.

Surplice A loose, white, knee-length garment worn over a longer garment by priests and members of the choir in some churches.

Surryfunge To rush around cleaning when company is on their way over.

Surtout A man's overcoat similar to a frock coat; cf. frock.

Susurrate To make a whispering or rustling sound.

Sutler A person who follows an army and sells provisions to the soldiers.

Swag A curtain or piece of fabric fastened to hang in a drooping curve; money or goods taken by a thief.

Swain A young lover or suitor; a country youth.

Swan of Avon   A nickname for Shakespeare who was born on the River Avon in Stratford and the ancient Greeks believed the souls of poets passed into swans.

Sward   An expanse of short grass.

Swinburnian   Relating to Charles Swinburne, an English philosopher and writer who dealt with controversial topics such as arguments for the existence of God.

Swineherd   A person who tends pigs.

Sybil   Any of certain women of antiquity reputed to possess powers of prophecy or divination; a female prophet or witch.

Symplegades   In Greek mythology, a pair of rocks at the Bosphorus that clashed together whenever a vessel went through, also called the Cyanean Rocks.

Synchronic   Concerned with something, especially a language, as it exists at one point in time.

Synchrony   Simultaneous action, development or occurrence.

Syncope   Fainting; a sudden, temporary loss of consciousness.

Syncretism   The amalgamation of different religions, cultures or schools of thought; the merging of different words during the development of language.

Syndic   A government official in some countries; a business agent for certain universities and corporations.

Synecdoche *A word from ancient Greece* meaning *simultaneous understanding* and used contemporarily as a literary device in which a part of something is substituted for the whole, like *hired hand* for *worker.*

Synechiae Adhesions of the iris to ocular structures in the eye which can cause issues of aqueous blockage and pupil dilation.

Synedoche A figure of speech where a part is made to represent the whole or vise versa (e.g., "The Lions won the game" refers to Detroit's football team.

Synesthesia The production of a sense impression relating to one part of the body when another part of the body is stimulated; the splashing over of impressions from one sense modality to another.

Synomosias To take an oath together.

Synoptic Forming a general summary or synopsis; relating to the Synoptic Gospels.

Systole The phase of the heartbeat when the heart muscle contracts and pumps blood from the chambers into the arteries; cf. diastole.

T

Tabard   A sleeveless jerkin consisting only of front and back pieces with a hole for the head.

Tabatière   An attic window, skylight or roof window; a snuff or tobacco box.

Tableau   A group of models or motionless figures representing a scene from a story or from history.

Tachycardic   A fast heart rate; a rapid heartbeat that is out of proportion to the age and level of exertion.

Tacitean   Relating to or characteristics of the Roman historian Tacitus.

Tacitus   Done without words, silent, implied, hidden, concealed (as in Tacitean wilderness).

Taffeta   A fine, lustrous silk or similar synthetic fabric with a crisp texture.

Tagala   A person who plays tricks; a deceiver, cheat or fraud.

Tallow   A hard, fatty substance made from rendered animal fat used in making candles and soap.

Tam A tall, round, knitted cap usually brightly colored from Jamaica.

Tamale A Mexican dish of seasoned meat wrapped in cornmeal dough and steamed or baked in corn husks.

Tamarack A slender North American larch.

Tamarind Pods from an Indian tree used in medicine and cooking.

Tancred A Norman leader in the First Crusade.

Tang A strong taste, flavor or smell.

Tangle foot Intoxicating liquor, especially cheap whiskey.

Tantalus *In Greek legend,* the son of Zeus who stole metal from the Gods and was cursed to an eternal life of deprivation or nourishment.

Tantric Relating to the doctrines of Hindu or Buddhist tantras, and in particular mantras, meditation, and ritual.

Taper A slender candle.

Tapis A tapestry or richly decorated cloth, used as a hanging or cover.

Tarboosh A man's cap similar to a fez, typically red felt with a tassel at the top.

Tare A common vetch; *in biblical use,* an injurious weed resembling wheat; cf. vetch.

Targe A small, round shield used by Scottish Highlanders in the early modern period.

Tarheel A nickname for the U.S. state of North Carolina.

Tarn A small mountain lake.

Tarnal To be damned; a mild imprecation.

Tarpaulin A heavy-duty waterproof cloth, originally of tarred canvas; historically, a sailor's tarred or oilskin hat.

Tartarus In Greek mythology, the Titan's deep abyss that is used as a dungeon of torment and suffering for the wicked and where souls are judged after death and the wicked receive divine punishment; a place where the gods locked up their enemies.

Tartine Bread and butter with jam.

Tartuffe From Moliere, a religious hypocrite or hypocritical pretender to excellence of any kind.

Tassel A tuft of loosely hanging threads knotted at one end and attached for decorating clothing or furnishings.

Tasso To arrange, put in order.

Tattie Scottish for a potato.

Tattoo A military event where soldiers march.

Taunton A market town in southwest England and administrative center of Somerset.

Tawny An orange-brown or yellowish-brown color.

Taxi dancer A dancing partner available for a fee.

Tay Kettle.

Te deum *God, we praise you*, an expression of thanksgiving or exultation.

Tearaway A person who behaves in a wild or reckless manner.

Teche The Bayou Teche is a 125-mile waterway in Louisiana named because it twists and turns resembling a snake's movement.

Tempera A method of painting with pigments dispersed in an emulsion miscible with water or egg yolk in the 12th through 15th centuries when it began to give way to oils.

Tempora mutantur A Latin adage that refers to the changes brought about by the passage of time.

Temporize To avoid making a decision or committing oneself in order to gain time; to temporarily adopt a particular course in order to conform to the circumstances.

Temps perdu *In French,* lost time (examples include the need to make up for lost time, irretrievable lost youth), used in Shakespeare's *Remembrance of Things Past.*

Tempus fugit Time flies.

Tenantry The tenants of an estate.

Tendentious A tendency in favor of a particular point of view; biased.

Tephrosia A genus of flowering plants in the Fabaceae family.

Teratology The scientific study of congenital abnormalities and abnormal formations.

Tercet A poem consisting of three lines.

Tergiversation Evasion from straightforward action or a clear-cut statement, equivocation; desertion of a cause, position party, or faith.

Terminus ad quem The point at which something ends or finishes; an aim or goal; cf. terminus ante quem, terminus post quem.

Terminus ante quem The latest possible date for something to happen; cf. terminus post quem, terminus ad quem.

Terminus post quem The earliest possible date for something; cf. terminus ante quem, termus ad quem.

Terra incognita Unknown or unexplored territory.

Terrapin A small edible turtle with lozenge-shaped markings on its shell found in coastal marshes in the eastern US; a freshwater edible turtle.

Terraqueous Consisting or formed of land and water.

Terrazzo A flooring material consisting of marble set in concrete and polished to give a smooth surface.

Terreplein A level space where a battery of guns is mounted.

Terrine A meat, vegetable, or fish mixture that has been cooked and cooled, typically served in slices.

Tertium quid An unidentified third element in combination with two known ones associated with alchemy; Latin for third something.

Tessitura The range within which most notes of a vocal part fall.

Testudo A protective Roman screen formed by a body of troops holding their shields above their heads in such a way that the shields overlap.

Tetanoid Resembling tetanus or tetany.

Tetchy Bad-tempered, irritable.

Tête de pont A bridgehead.

Tethys *In Greek mythology*, the sea goddess and wife of Oceanus.

Tetrahedron A solid having four plane triangular faces; a triangular pyramid.

Tettix A cicada, especially in Greece.

Thanatopsis A meditation on death.

Thawra To rise up, to be stirred or excited; revolution.

Thebaid   The area near Thebes, Egypt, which was a center of Christian monasticism in the 4th century.

Theocritus   An ancient Greek poet from Sicily and creator of pastoral poetry.

Theodolite   A surveying instrument with a rotating telescope for measuring horizontal and vertical angles.

Theophany   *For Christians and Jews,* the manifestation of the Abrahamic God to people, the sensible sign by which his presence is revealed.

Theosophical   Refers to philosophies that maintain knowledge of God may be achieved through spiritual ecstasy, direct intuition, or special individual relations.

Theosophist   Any number of philosophies maintaining that knowledge of God may be achieved through spiritual ecstasy, direct intuition or special individual relations.

Theurgy   The operation or effect of a supernatural or divine agency in human affairs.

Thickset   Heavily or solidly built; stocky.

Thimblerigger   A swindling trick in which a small ball is quickly shifted from under one to another of the three small cups to fool the spectator into guessing its location.

Thoroughbred   A horse of a pure breed widely used in racing; cf. purebred.

Thralldom   The state of being a thrall; bondage, slavery, servitude; cf. thrall.

Thrall   The state of being in someone's power or having great power over someone; a slave, servant or captive; cf. enthralled.

Threnody   A lament.

Throve   Past tense of to thrive, to prosper, to flourish.

Thurible   A metal censer suspended from chains in which incense is burned during worship services.

Thyme   A low-growing, aromatic plant with small leaves of the mint family used as a culinary herb and medicinal oil.

Thymy   A low-growing aromatic plant of the mint family with small leaves used as a culinary herb and in medicine.

Thyrsus   *In ancient Greece and Rome*, a staff or spear tipped with an ornament.

Tiara   A jeweled ornamental band worn on the front of a woman's hair.

Tierce   Three parts; also spelling for terce, a service forming part of Christianity said or chanted the third hour of the day (i.e., 9 a.m.).

Tiffin   A light meal, especially lunch.

Tilde   The symbol ~ which came into English from Spanish, meaning title.

Tiller   A horizontal bar fitted to the head of a boat's rudder used as a lever for steering.

Tilth   Cultivation of land; tillage; the condition of tilled soil; prepared surface soil.

Timorous   Showing nervousness, fear, or lack of confidence; timid.

Tine   A prong or sharp point such as that on a fork or antler.

Tinker   A person who travels from place to place mending metal utensils as a way of making a living.

Tintinnabulation   The lingering sound of a ringing bell that occurs after the bell has been stuck, a word coined by poet Edgar Allan Poe.

Tippet   A cape.

Tipple   To drink alcohol, especially habitually.

Tischwein   Table wine.

Tithe   One-tenth part of something, paid as a contribution to a religious organization or compulsory tax to government; cf. tithing.

Tither   A person who gives tithes to a church; a person who advocates payment of tithes.

Titter   A short, half-suppressed laugh; a giggle.

Tittle   The dot over an i or j.

Tmesis   The separation of parts of a compound word with intervening words, usually in informal speech, e.g. "a whole nother story."

Toff A rich or upper-class person.

Toffy A firm, hard candy that softens when sucked or chewed.

Toggle A small piece of wood or plastic that is used as a button on clothing.

Toile An early version of a finished garment made of cheap material so the design can be tested and perfected; a translucent linen or cotton fabric used for making clothes.

Toilette A small piece of cloth put over the shoulders while dressing the hair or shaving.

Toise An old French length of about six feet.

Tonguey Fluent or voluble in speech, loquacious, garrulous; having the characteristics of a tongue.

Tong war A series of violent disputes beginning in the late 19th century among rival Chinese.

Tong Factions centered in Chinatowns of various American cities, and in particular, San Francisco.

Tonneau The area of a car or truck open at the back which can be used for passengers or cargo; a cover that spans the back of a pickup truck.

Tontine An investment that provides an income to a living person for as long as that person is alive.

Toper A drunkard; to drink heavily.

Topgallant The section of a square-rigged sailing ship's mast above the topmast.

Topi A hat, especially a sola topi; cf. sola topi.

Topos A traditional theme or formula in literature.

Topper A silk hat; an opera hat; a woman's short and loose-fitting lightweight outer coat.

Tory British political party for traditions and conservatism, of upholding the social order as it has evolved in English history (cf. Whig).

Totem A person or thing regarded as being symbolic of a quality or concept; an emblem or badge that features an animal or plant.

Totemic Resembling a totem; regarded as being symbolic or representative of a particular quality or concept.

Totemism The belief that humans have a mystical relationship with a spirit being such as an animal or plant characterized in a totem as a symbol or emblem.

Tot To add up numbers or amounts.

Toucan A tropical American brightly colored plumage fruit-eating bird with a massive bill.

Tout court Quite short, brusque or simply, as in tout court speech or a very short and to-the-point speech.

Tout simplement *French for* just like that, or without any warning.

Tout To offer racing tips for a share of any resulting winnings.

Tower of Siloam An ancient Greek structure that fell killing 18 people which, in the Gospel of Luke, Jesus uses to describe the need for individual repentance for sin.

Tow-row A noisy outburst, racket, rumpus.

Toxophilite An archer.

Trace A fort with projecting angles.

Trace-chain A long, strong chain which is attached to a line of draft animals, usually by whiffletrees; cf. whiffletree.

Trace-horse An extra horse hitched beside a team to assist in drawing a load through a difficult spot like up an incline.

Traces A narrow track made along the alignment of a hill or road to enable inspection.

Tract A definite region or area of the body, especially a group, series, or system of related parts or organs, e.g., the digestive tract.

Tractarianism A 19th-century movement that sought to renew Roman Catholicism in England, also known as the Oxford Movement because it was centered in Oxford.

Traipses To walk or move wearily or reluctantly; to walk or go aimlessly without finding or reaching one's goals; a tedious or tiring journey on foot; archaic for a slovenly woman.

Tranche A portion of something, especially money; in finance, one of several related securities offered as part of the same transaction.

Transcaspian The name used in the second half of the 19th century for the section of the Russian Empire to the east of the Caspian Sea
.

Transept In a cross-shaped church, either of the two parts forming the arms of the cross-shape projecting at right angles from the nave.

Transliteration To represent or spell in the characters of another alphabet.

Transpicuous Transparent; easily understood, lucid.

Tranter Someone who sells goods while traveling from place to place; a peddler.

Trattoria An Italian restaurant serving simple food.

Travertine White or light-colored calcareous rock deposited from mineral springs used in building.

Treacle A thick, sticky dark syrup made from refined sugar; molasses; cloying sentimentality or flattery.

Treacly Excessively sentimental.

Trefoil A small European plant of the pea family with yellow flowers and three-lobed, clover- like leaves.

Trencherman A person who eats in a specified manner, typically heartily.

Trepak   A fiery Ukrainian folk dance performed by men featuring the leg-flinging prisiadka; cf. prisiadka.

Trews   Close-fitting tartan trousers worn by certain Scottish regiments; trousers.

Triad   A set of three connected people or things; a secret crime society in China.

Tribe   A group of related animals or plants.

Tribrachic   A metrical foot of three short syllables of which two belong to the thesis and one to the arsis; cf. arsis.

Trice   To haul up or in and lash or secure with a small rope, like a sail.

Trident   A three-pronged spear, especially as an attribute to Poseidon (Neptune) or Britannia.

Triennial   Occurring every three years.

Triforium   A gallery or arcade above the arches of the nave, choir and transepts of a church.

Trill   A quavering or vibratory sound, especially a rapid alteration of sung and or played notes; to produce a quavering or warbling sound.

Trinitarian   Relating to the belief in the doctrine of the Trinity.

Tripe   Nonsense, rubbish; the first or second stomach of a cow.

Tripod A stool, table, or cauldron resting on three legs.

Triptych A picture or relief carving on three panels typically hinged together side by side and used as an altarpiece.

Triste Sad, mournful; wistful.

Tristram A Welsh word that means noise or chatter with the additional meaning of bold.

Trivium *In ancient education,* consisting of grammar, logic, and rhetoric; cf. quadrivium.

Trochaic A pattern in poetry that features trochees; cf. trochee.

Trochee A foot consisting of one long syllable followed by one short syllable: cf. iamb; cf. trochaic.

Trollop A woman who has many casual sexual encounters or relationships; a female prostitute.

Troll To leave an insulting or offensive message on the Internet to upset someone.

Trompe l'oeil Visual illusion in art, especially to trick the eye into perceiving as a three-dimensional object.

Trope A figurative or metaphorical use of a word or expression such as *stop and smell the roses.*

Trottant To trot.

Trouvaille A lucky find.

Truckle A small barrel-shaped cheese, especially Cheddar.

Truck Trash or rubbish; to not deal with.

Trussed Having had the wings and legs tied before cooking, like a bird.

Tubercle A small, rounded projection or protuberance, especially on a bone or the surface of an animal or plant; a small nodular lesion in the lungs characteristic of tuberculosis.

Tuche The rear pelvic area of the human body, the buttocks.

Tufaa *Latin for* concrete.

Tuft A bunch or collection of threads, grass, hair, etc., held together at the base; c. f. tufted.

Tufted To provide or adorn with a tuft; to make something firm by stitching at intervals and covering the depressions produced with tufts; cf. tuft.

Tugendbund A German patriotic league founded in 1808 dedicated to the overthrow of Napoleon; a 19th-century man's boot reaching above the knee in front with a piece cut out behind, originally worn by cavalrymen.

Tumescence Swollen or becoming swollen, especially as a response to sexual arousal; pompous or pretentious language; cf. detumescence.

Tunny A tuna, especially a Bluefin.

Turbot A European inshore flatfish with large bony tubercles prized as food.

Tureen A deep-covered dish from which soup is served.

Turlet Slang for toilet.

Turnstile A device that controls the way into or out of a building, room, or area of land, especially one that you have to pay to enter.

Turnuse The eastern tiger swallowtail, a butterfly of eastern North America.

Twattle To gossip.

Twilled Fabric woven to have a surface of diagonal, parallel ridges.

Twilt A quilt.

Twitted To tease or taunt someone, especially in a good-humored way.

Twitter-light Twilight.

Twit To taunt, tease, or ridicule; to gibe at.

Two penny Consisting of, or worth British two pence.

Two-fer An item or offer that comprises two items but is sold for the price of one.

Tyche *In Greek religion,* the goddess of chance, the capricious dispenser of good or ill fortune, later identified with the Roman goddess Fortuna.

Tympanum   *In architecture,* a semicircular or triangular decorative wall surface over an entrance, door or window bounded by a lintel and an arch; the tympanic membrane or eardrum.

Typology   A classification according to general type; the study and interpretation of types and symbols, especially in the Bible.

Tyrian   Relating to or characteristic of the Lebanese port of Tyre.

U

Ulema A body of Muslim scholars recognized as having specialized knowledge of Islamic sacred law and theology.

Ulster A man's loose overcoat of rough cloth typically with a belt at the back.

Ultrabasic Relating to igneous rocks having silica content less than 45% by weight, most of which is ultramafic; cf. ultramafic.

Ultramafic Relating to igneous rocks composed of mafic materials; cf. ultrabasic.

Ultramarine A brilliant, deep-blue pigment.

Ultramontanism Advocating supreme papal authority in faith and discipline; a person advocating supreme papal authority; situated on the other side of the Alps from the point of view of the speaker.

Umbricius To be petty, greedy, and jealous.

Umlaut A mark (ë) used over a vowel to indicate a different vowel quality.

Unbolted Not sifted, not having the bran or coarse part separated by a bolter; hence coarse, gross, unrefined.

Uneeda A girl's name meaning to have talent, charm, and luck.

Unfrock To defrock; cf. defrock.

Unguent A soft greasy or viscous substance used as ointment or lubrication.

Uniformitarianism *In geology*, the theory that changes in the earth's crust during geological history have resulted from the action of continuous and uniform processes.

Unpent Not pent up, unconfined; released; cf. pent.

Unprepossessing Not particularly attractive or appealing to the eye.

Unx vomica A spiny southern Asian tree with orange fruit and toxic seeds that are a commercial source of strychnine, also known as the strychnine tree.

Upborne To bear up; raise aloft; sustain or support.

Uraeus A representation of a sacred serpent as an emblem of supreme power, worn on the headdresses of ancient Egyptian deities and sovereigns.

Uremia A raised level of urea in the blood that is normally eliminated by the kidneys.

Ut pictura poesis *As is painting, so is poetry*, or *poetry is like painting*.

V

Vagitus   The cry of a newborn baby.

Vale of Tears   *A Christian phrase*, referring to the tribulations of life Christian doctrine says are left behind only when one leaves this world and enters Heaven.

Valedictory   Serving as a farewell.

Valence   *In psychology*, a quality referring to intrinsic goodness (positive valence) or badness (negative valence) of an object, event, or situation.

Valerian   A perennial, flowering plant native to Europe and Asia.

Valetudinarian   A person who is unduly anxious about their health.

Valhalla   *In Norse mythology*, the hall of slain warriors who live blissfully under the leadership of the god Odin, depicted as a splendid palace roofed with shields where the warriors feast and are made whole again each evening.

Valiance   Valor; the qualities of a hero or heroine; exceptional courage when faced with danger.

Valspar   The first ever clear varnish.

Vamp The part of a shoe that covers the top of the foot.

Vandalic Relating to or characteristic of the Vandals.

Vapourish A fanciful mood.

Vaquero A cowboy; a cattle-driver.

Var A value-added reseller, a company that adds extra features to products for resale; a method of quantifying the risk of holding a financial asset.

Variegation A diversity of colors.

Varioloid A mild form of smallpox.

Vasculature The vascular system of a part of the body and its arrangement.

Vates A prophet or poet; a poet or bard who is divinely inspired.

Vatic Describing or predicting what will happen in the future.

Veal Pen An individual's cube in the feedlot that is corporate America, as an unsuspecting worker kept in the dark, restricted, and controlled.

Vection The sensation of movement of the body in space produced purely by visual stimulation.

Vedette A mounted sentry positioned beyond an army's outposts to observe the movements of the enemy; a leading star of stage, screen, or television.

Velarium   The canvas that covers the coliseum in Rome.

Veldt   Open, uncultivated country or grassland in southern Africa.

Vellum   Fine parchment made from the skin of a calf; smooth writing paper imitating vellum.

Velveteen   A cotton fabric with a pile resembling velvet; trousers made of velveteen.

Vend   To offer for sale, especially from a stall or slot machine.

Venireman   Persons who form a venire; prospective jurors; cf. venire.

Venire   The entire panel from which a jury is drawn; cf. venireman.

Venter   The underside or abdomen of an animal.

Verba visibilia   Visible words.

Verdure   Lush green vegetation; a condition of freshness.

Verger   A church caretaker or attendant; an officer of the church who carries a rod before a bishop or dean as a symbol of office.

Verge   The shoulder of a road.

Veridical   Not illusory.

Vermilion   A brilliant red pigment made from mercury sulfide.

Verres   A rapacious and corrupt provincial administrator.

Vers libre   Free verse in French, refers to the 19th century poetic innovation that liberated French poetry from its traditional prosodic rules.

Versace   Gianni Versace, an Italian fashion designer; someone who designs clothing.

Verso   The left or back side of an open book; cf. recto.

Verve   Vigor and spirit or enthusiasm.

Vestal   A female virgin, a woman who has never had sexual relations.

Vestment   A chasuble or other robe worn by the clergy during services.

Vestry   A room or building attached to a church used as an office and for changing into vestments; a meeting of parishioners for the conduct of parochial business; a body of parishioners meeting in a vestry.

Vetch   A scrambling herbaceous plant of the pea family cultivated as silage or fodder crop; cf. tare.

Via crucis   A lengthy and distressing or painful procedure.

Vilipending   To be disparaging.

Villanelle   A nineteen-line poem with two rhymes throughout.

Villein   *In medieval times,* a feudal tenant entirely subject to a lord to whom they pay dues and services in return for land.

Vingt et un   A gambling game using cards, also called twenty-one.

Vinous   Related to wine; to be fond of wine; the reddish color of wine.

Vipère   A viper; a venomous snake with large, hinged fangs.

Virchowian   A form of leprosy in which patients are without fever and nodules but with shiny skin.

Virgulia divina   A Y-shaped twig or rod called a divining rod to find water.

Viscount   One of five ranks of British nobility which are, in ascending order, Duke, Marquis, Earl, Viscount and Baron; the Viscount assists courts in their running provinces and often takes judicial responsibility; cf. Duke, Marquis, Earl and Baron.

Vittae   *In Botany,* an oil tube in the fruit of some plants; *in Zoology,* a band or stripe of color.

Viva voce   Oral rather than written; an oral examination, typically for an academic qualification.

Vivarium   An enclosure, container, or structure for keeping animals under seminatural conditions for observation, study or pets.

Viz *Latin for* videlicet meaning "namely," "that is to say" or "in other words."

Vizier A high official in some Muslim countries, especially in Turkey under Ottoman rule.

Vocables Meaningless lyrics to a song, like "na, na, na."

Vocalic Relating to or consisting of a vowel.

Vol au vent A small, round pastry filled with a savory mixture, typically meat or fish in a richly flavored sauce.

Vole A small, mouse-like rodent with a rounded muzzle found in Eurasia and North America.

Volkssprache Everyday language, vernacular.

Volute A spiral scroll characteristic of Ironic capitals and also used in Corinthian and composite capitals; cf. capital.

Vorticism A British artistic movement of 1914-15 favoring harsh, angular, machine-like forms.

Votary A person who has made vows of dedication to religious service; a devoted follower, adherent, or advocate.

Votive Something offered or consecrated in fulfillment of a vow.

Vouchsafe To grant or furnish graciously or condescendingly; to grant as a privilege or special favor.

Voussoir   A wedged-shaped or tapered stone used to construct an arch.

Vox dei   The voice of God.

Vox populi   The opinions or beliefs of the majority; the voice of the people.

Vraie vérité   The real truth.

Vulgate   Common or colloquial speech; the principal Latin version of the *Bible*, prepared mainly by St. Jerome in the late-4th century and adopted as the official text for the Roman Catholic Church.

Vulpine   Relating to foxes; crafty, cunning.

W

Wabbly Same as wobbly, to tremble, quaver, waver or vacillate.

Wafer A gummed seal for letters.

Waggish Mischief, playful, innocent & reckless behavior.

Walcheren ague An epidemic.

Wale A ridge on a textured woven fabric such as corduroy; a thick plank running along the side of a wooden ship used to strengthen and protect the hull.

Wall-eyed A disorder in which the eyes don't look exactly in the same direction at the same time.

Wamble The rumblings of the stomach.

Wampum Small cylindrical beads made by North American Indians from shells strung together and worn as decoration or used as money.

Wan A pale appearance giving the impression of illness or exhaustion; pale, weak.

Wane To decrease in strength, intensity; cf. wax.

Wan face Having a pale or sickly color; showing little effort or energy, as in a wan smile; weak.

Ware pottery Typically a special kind; manufactured articles of a specified type; articles offered for sale.

Warped Abnormal or strange, distorted.

Wassermann A German bacteriologist who developed a diagnostic test for syphilis.

Wat A Buddhist monastery or temple.

Water pipe A pipe for smoking tobacco, cannabis etc., that draws the smoke through water to cool it.

Water butt A large container for collecting rainwater that can be used to water plants, a rain barrel.

Wattle Material for making things like fences and walls consisting of rods or stakes interlaced with twigs or branches.

Wax To grow larger, increase; cf. wane.

Way Bill A list of passengers or goods being carried on a vehicle.

Waylay To stop or interrupt someone and detain them in conversation or to trouble in some other way.

Weald A heavily wooded area; a forest.

Wearing To make tired or annoyed.

Welkin The sky or heaven.

Wen   A boil, swelling or growth on the skin; an outstandingly large or overcrowded city.

Wend   To move slowly and not directly; to direct one's course; to travel.

Werrie   Another spelling of weary.

Wettliteratur   A term coined by Goethe to suggest the capacity of literature to transcend national and linguistic boundaries, world literature.

Wheat pit   A market or exchange where wheat stocks are bought and sold.

Wheedle   To use flattery or coaxing in order to persuade someone to do something or give one something.

Whelk   A predatory marine mollusk with a heavy, pointed spiral shell some of which are edible.

Wherry   A light rowboat used chiefly for carrying passengers; a large light barge.

Whiffletree   A mechanism to distribute force evenly through linkages consisting of a bar pivoted at the center with force applied from numerous directions to the pivot that usually connects many draft animals.

Whig   A British political party of the late 17th through early 19th centuries seeking to limit royal authority and increase parliamentary power (cf. Tory); an American favoring independence from Great Britain during the American Revolution.

Whilom   Formerly, in the past; erstwhile.

Whisker   Poles used to "wing out" the jib when sailing downwind; a thin strand of metal that grows out of the original shape of a metal.

Whistly   To make a whistling sound.

White wing   A person and especially a street sweeper wearing a white uniform.

Whom   The receiver of the action (whom do you like best); cf. who.

Who   The doer in the action (the one who scored the goal); cf. whom.

Wick   A little harbor.

Widdendream   A state of mental confusion or excitement.

Widdershins   In a direction contrary to the sun's course, considered unlucky; counterclockwise.

Wienerwurst   A smoked pork or beef sausage similar to a frankfurter.

Wilderman   An elaboration of wild.

Wirepuller   A person, especially a politician, who exerts control or influence from behind the scenes.

Wither   The ridge between the shoulder bones of a horse.

Wobblies   Members of the Industrial Workers of the World.

Wold *In Britain,* a piece of high, open, uncultivated land or moor; cf. moor, heath.

Woolgathering The act of gathering tufts of sheep wool; indulgence in aimless thought or dreamy imagining; absentmindedness.

Woolly Made of wool; vague or confused in expression or character, wooly thinking.

Wop An offensive term for an Italian or other southern European.

Worm Fence A zigzag fence consisting of interlocking rails supported by crossed poles, also called a snake or Virginia fence.

Worsted A fine, smooth yarn spun from combed long-staple wool.

Wot Nonstandard spelling of what.

Wrapper A loose dressing gown for women like a housecoat or negligee.

Writ A legal document that contains a written order instructing someone to do something or to stop doing something.

Wrought Archaic for to work; to mold, shape, or manufacture.

Wugwump A woman with a mustache.

Wust Desolate, waste; an indefinite quantity that is above the average in size or magnitude.

John L. Bowman

X-Y-Z

Xylographic   The art of making engravings on wood, especially for printing.

Yam   The edible, starchy tuber of a climbing plant widely grown in tropical and subtropical countries.

Yarb   An herb.

Yawning   Wide open, cavernous.

Yawp   To utter a loud, harsh cry; to yelp, squawk, or bawl; to talk noisily and foolishly or complainingly.

Yegg   Safecracker; a burglar; cf. yeggmen.

Yeggman   A person who breaks open safes; a yegg; cf. yegg.

Yerba   An evergreen tree cultivated for its leaves which contain caffeine; a stimulating milky beverage made from the dried leaves of this tree.

Yokelry   Gullible, unsophisticated country folk.

Zarzuela   A Spanish traditional form of musical comedy; a Spanish dish of various kinds of seafood cooked in a rich sauce.

Zeitgeber A time giver or synchronizer.

Zeuxis Famous Greek painter who flourished during the 5th century B.C. known for his ability to imitate nature and still life.

Zic-zac To cause to move in or to form a zigzag.

Zigaro A noun that describes reality and names things like people, objects and sensations.

Zoomorphic Having or representing animal forms or gods as animal forms.

Zouave A member of French light infantry corps; woman's trousers with wide tops tapering to a narrow ankle.

Zwieback A rusk or cracker made by baking a small loaf and then toasting slices until they are dry and crisp; cf. rusk.

Zymosis The process in which an agent causes an organic substance to break down into simpler substances; an infection or a contagious disease.

www.ingramcontent.com/pod-product-compliance
Lightning Source LLC
Chambersburg PA
CBHW070056030426
42335CB00016B/1910